D1194012

The Scarecrow Author Bibliographies

1. John Steinbeck (Tetsumaro Hayashi). 1973.
2. Joseph Conrad (Theodore G. Ehrsam). 1969.
3. Arthur Miller (Tetsumaro Hayashi). 2d ed. due 1976.
4. Katherine Anne Porter (Waldrip & Bauer). 1969.
5. Philip Freneau (Philip M. Marsh). 1970.
6. Robert Greene (Tetsumaro Hayashi). 1971.
7. Benjamin Disraeli (R. W. Stewart). 1972.
8. John Berryman (Richard W. Kelly). 1972.
9. William Dean Howells (Vito J. Brenñi). 1973.
10. Jean Anouilh (Kathleen W. Kelly). 1973.
11. E. M. Forster (Alfred Borrello). 1973.
12. The Marquis de Sade (E. Pierre Chanover). 1973.
13. Alain Robbe-Grillet (Dale W. Fraizer). 1973.
14. Northrop Frye (Robert D. Denham). 1974.
15. Federico García Lorca (Laurenti & Siracusa). 1974.
16. Ben Jonson (Brock & Welsh). 1974.
17. Four French Dramatists: Eugène Brieux, François de Curel, Emile Fabre, Paul Hervieu (Edmund F. SantaVicca). 1974.
18. Ralph Waldo Ellison (Jacqueline Covo). 1974.
19. Philip Roth (Bernard F. Rodgers, Jr.). 1974.
20. Norman Mailer (Laura Adams). 1974.
21. Sir John Betjeman (Margaret Stapleton). 1974.
22. Elie Wiesel (Molly Abramowitz). 1974.
23. Paul Laurence Dunbar (Eugene W. Metcalf, Jr.). 1975.
24. Henry James (Beatrice Ricks). 1975.
25. Robert Frost (Lentricchia & Lentricchia). 1976.
26. Sherwood Anderson (Douglas G. Rogers). 1976.
27. Iris Murdoch and Muriel Spark (Tominaga and Schneidermeyer). 1976.
28. John Ruskin (Kirk H. Beetz). 1976.
29. Georges Simenon (Trudee Young). 1976.

SHERWOOD ANDERSON:

A Selective, Annotated Bibliography

by

Douglas G. Rogers

The Scarecrow Author Bibliographies, No. 26

The Scarecrow Press, Inc.

Metuchen, N.J.   1976

Library of Congress Cataloging in Publication Data

Rogers, Douglas G   1948-
    Sherwood Anderson : a selective, annotated biblio-
graphy.

    (The Scarecrow author bibliographies ; no. 26)
    Bibliography: p.
    Includes index.
    1. Anderson, Sherwood, 1876-1941--Bibliography.
Z8035.6.R63   [PS3501.N4]   016.813'5'2   75-45225
ISBN 0-8108-0900-1

For
David D. Anderson and Ray Lewis White,
scholars to whom all students
of Anderson are deeply indebted

CONTENTS

INTRODUCTION

The year 1976 marks Sherwood Anderson's centenary, and Michigan State University will host a three-day Commemorative Conference in September. Events at the conference will include: 1) a dramatic sequence with a reading of Anderson's poetry, a stage presentation of "The Triumph of the Egg," and the PBS production of Winesburg, Ohio; 2) discussions, panels, and featured speakers; 3) scholarly papers; and 4) exhibits of photos, works, criticisms, and biography. In addition American Notes and Queries will devote its September issue to critical, biographical, and bibliographical notes on Anderson; Professors Hilbert H. Campbell and Charles E. Modlin will edit a supplementary volume to the special AN&Q issue, and David D. Anderson plans to publish a volume of essays entitled Sherwood Anderson: The Dimensions of his Literary Art. Welford D. Taylor from the University of Richmond is currently spearheading the formation of the Sherwood Anderson Society, and it is likely that Walter B. Rideout's long-awaited biography of Anderson will see the light of day. All of this scholarly activity is being focused upon the centennial celebration of a man who has been labeled by one of his biographers a distinctly minor figure,[1] but a man who nonetheless occupies a most distinct position in the history of American letters. In order to justify this pinnacle of critical interest in Anderson, it is necessary to survey the history of Anderson the man and, more importantly, to examine Anderson's literary career from the publication of his first novel, Windy McPherson's Son, until his death in 1941.

Sherwood Anderson was born in Camden, Ohio, on September 13, 1876. His father, Irwin Anderson, had served as a cavalryman in the Civil War and earned his living as a harnessmaker. His mother, Emma Smith Anderson, a former serving girl, married Irwin when she was twenty. Both parents play significant roles in Anderson's later fiction as Anderson sought to understand his relationship to them, but often there is a wide discrepancy between the facts of their

1

lives and Anderson's fictional portrayal of them.

Anderson grew up in Clyde, Ohio, where his family had settled after living in Camden and for a short time in Caledonia. Irwin Anderson had fallen victim to the on-rushing machine age that gradually displaced many skilled craftsmen in the late nineteenth century. With business in his own shop falling off, Irwin was reduced to working as a hired hand in the Ervin Brothers' harness shop. But within a year, he lost his job and began a career as a sign and house painter--a vocation that provided weak and irregular support for his family of eight. In almost pathetic response to the cruel joke a changing America had played upon him, Irwin Anderson increasingly sought escape in storytelling and drinking. Anderson grew to hate his father for his irresponsibility, and his hatred was sharpened by the shame he felt at his mother's role as town washerwoman. In an attempt to increase the family income, Emma Anderson took in washing. Sherwood was deeply distressed by his mother's hard work and always remembered "a kind of shame that began to grow in the breasts of us children when we were sent off to bear home baskets of dirty clothes or to return them washed and ironed. "

With Irwin proving an unsteady provider, Anderson's elder sister Stella helped support the family by teaching school, and each of the boys contributed by working at odd jobs. Though the Anderson home was not so desperately poverty-stricken[2] as Anderson would later depict it, it could not satisfy the needs and desires of young Sherwood, who earned the nickname "Jobby" from his aggressive willingness to work hard and earn money.

Anderson grew to young manhood in Clyde, Ohio. He dropped out of high school to work in a local bicycle manufacturing company and at age nineteen joined a local unit of the National Guard. In May, 1895, Emma Anderson, exhausted by overwork and tuberculosis, died, and less than a year later Sherwood left Clyde to seek his fortune in the windy city, Chicago. He spent about a year and a half in Chicago rolling barrels of apples in a cold-storage warehouse. In 1898, Anderson left Chicago to join Company I, the Sixth Ohio Regiment of Volunteer Infantry. After four months of non-combat duty as part of the occupation forces in Cuba, Corporal Sherwood Anderson was honorably discharged in May, 1899.

After a brief return to Clyde, Sherwood traveled to

Springfield, Ohio, where he lived in a boarding house with
his brother Karl and completed his high school education at
Wittenberg Academy. He graduated from Wittenberg in June,
1900, and delivered a commencement address on Zionism.
Impressed by Anderson's oration, Harry Simmons, an advertising executive for The Woman's Home Companion, offered Sherwood a job in the magazine's Chicago office. Dis-
liked by his superior in the Crowell office, Anderson soon
moved to the Frank White agency where he worked as a copywriter. After the firm's merger with the Long-Critchfield
Company, Anderson also traveled and solicited accounts, for
which he wrote the copy.

During 1903 and 1904 Anderson wrote numerous articles for Agricultural Advertising. His two signed columns,
"Rot and Reason" and "Business Types," show Anderson's
sincere championing of the business ethic. In one article he
frankly states that business can know only one kind of success, and that is making money. Anderson was to spend
most of his later literary life rebelling against the money-
oriented Anderson of his youth.

In the fall of 1906 Anderson left his position at Long-
Critchfield to assume the presidency of the United Factories
Company in Cleveland, Ohio. The company, a mail-order
outlet for several manufacturers, encountered serious difficulties arising from the sale of defective incubators. In late
1907, Anderson left Cleveland and started a mail-order paint
company in Elyria, Ohio. In 1908, the successful Anderson
Manufacturing Company began to produce its own paint.

Anderson had married Cornelia Lane in 1904, and by
1911 had fathered three children. Yet despite his business
and family success, Anderson grew more and more dissatisfied with the state of his life. Disenchanted with the business world, he leaned increasingly toward the world of books.
As he writes in his Memoirs, "a curious sickness came. I
had always been a passionate reader. It may be that I began
to get through my reading of the words of great men, a new
conception of what a man's life might be. "[3] Anderson sought
to relieve his unhappiness by increasing his work load, golfing,
drinking, and running about with women. When these activities failed to alleviate his disenchantment, Anderson turned
to writing. Claiming an attic room in his home as private
and off-limits to the rest of his family, Anderson sought fulfillment in placing words on paper. Working furtively in his
attic sanctuary, Anderson produced five lengthy books--four

novels and a destroyed book entitled Why I Am a Socialist.
Two of the novel manuscripts--Mary Cochran and Talbot
Whittingham--survive only as fragments.   They, along with
the manuscript of Marching Men, are housed in the Anderson
collection at the Newberry Library.   The manuscript of Windy
McPherson's Son is not known to have survived.

The pressure of living in two worlds--the creative
world of his own literature and the demanding world of busi-
ness--was too difficult for Anderson to bear.   In November,
1912, the incident occurred that gave birth to the Anderson
myth.   The myth--that Anderson consciously and abruptly
abandoned the business life with its inherent emphasis on
making money to assume the life of the artist--has been per-
petuated by Anderson and his admirers who prefer the spirit
to the essence of the truth.   As Anderson later remembered
the event, his departure from Elyria came as a moment of
mystical truth.   Stopping suddenly in the midst of dictating
a letter to his secretary, Anderson announced, "My feet are
cold, wet, and heavy from long walking in a river.   Now I
shall go walk on dry land. "[4]   Minutes later, he walked out
of the factory and for four days wandered about aimlessly
until he was found dazed and suffering from nervous exhaustion in Cleveland on December 1st.   A letter mailed on November 30th by Anderson to his wife Cornelia suggests that
Anderson was suffering a kind of amnesia and that his exit
from Elyria was psychologically akin to escape from his role
as an adult business male. [5]

On February 16, 1913, the Elyria Democrat noted that
Anderson had decided to return to Chicago to resume work
with the Taylor-Critchfield Advertising Company.   Sherwood
Anderson was thirty-six when he left Elyria.   He was to earn
his living as an advertising copywriter, but he carried with
him the manuscripts of his early novels and the hope that he
would someday be able to devote all his energies to the writing of fiction.

In 1916, Anderson signed a contract to publish three
books with the John Lane publishing house.   He had secured
the contract on the merits of his Windy McPherson manuscript and the combined influence of Floyd Dell and Theodore
Dreiser.   Essentially, Windy McPherson's Son is the story
of a poor, small-town boy who, through industry and wit,
rises to a position of wealth and power in the city of Chicago.
As Wright Morris has pointed out, "writers of substance give
us something of their measure, and their enduring preoccupa-

tions, in the first book they publish, and McPherson is no
exception."6 Sam McPherson's search for truth and rejection of the money-making business world parallels Anderson's
own rejection of materialistic standards in Ohio. The theme
that dominates the novel recurs in Anderson's later fiction--
as a sensitive human being, he is concerned with the reten-
tion of human dignity and the search for lasting values in the
face of a brutal, materialistic universe. Reviewers of the
novel were quick to spot its flaws. Francis Hackett found
it marred by lengthy expression of those "thoughts which so
enamor the young novelist,"7 and Waldo Frank recognized the
static, unsatisfactory ending. However, each of these reviewers also recognized Anderson's potential genius, and
noted that he had touched upon essential truths in the American experience. Hackett, who particularly appreciated the
mass of midwestern humanity that people the book, believed
that Anderson had "made the America of the small town his
own, its stridencies and heart-hungers and thin spiral fires."8
And Waldo Frank admiringly observed that despite the puerile,
fumbling flaws, "through it all is a radiant glow of truth."9

The Lane Company published Anderson's second novel,
Marching Men, in 1917. The book received only scant attention, with total sales reaching about one thousand copies.
An experience in Anderson's military training may have gen-
erated the idea for Marching Men. Anderson recalls having
dropped out of a company marching drill to remove a stone
from his shoe. Watching his comrades from the edge of a
woods, he observes,

> We had been marching for hours, I was not weary.
> It seemed to me, that day, that into my legs had
> come the strength of the legs of thirty thousand
> men. I had become a giant.... I remember that
> later, when I got back to camp, I did not want to
> speak to others.... I was a man in love. I was
> in love with the thought of the possibilities of my-
> self combined with others.10

A later incident in Chicago may have reinforced the
central theme of Marching Men.

> I was in Chicago and stood on the station of the
> elevated railroad. It was evening and people were
> pouring out of offices and stores. They came by
> thousands out of side streets and into the broad
> city street of faces. They were a broken mob.

They did not keep step. There were thousands of
individuals, lost like myself. As individuals, they
had no strength, no courage. 11

    Beaut McGregor, the protagonist of Marching Men,
moves from a hatred for the people in the tiny Pennsylvania
mining town where he is raised, to a love for these people
and a redirected hatred for the materialistic society that attacks man's freedom and dignity. Endowed with Anderson's
vision of the strength of unity and the power of men marching together, McGregor attempts to fight the exploitation of
capitalist employers by leading the miners in a marching
movement. The novel ends with the implication that McGreg-
or and his movement will not succeed, but Anderson asserts
through McGregor an element of human dignity in the face of
overwhelming industrial power. Understandably, critics perceived the book as eminently pro-labor, a "proletarian novel. "12 They noted, too, the obvious weakness of the second
half of the novel and the technical strain of forcing McGregor
into a kind of primordial hero role. But Anderson's novel
was ultimately saved from critical damnation by an accurate
and sensitive vision that captures a "freshness of feeling about
workingmen and women, the vividly frank and abrupt opinions,
the flashes of energetic description, ... the details of mining-
town and apple-warehouse and night restaurant and Chicago
pulchritude, the reminiscence of 1893 and of First Ward infamies, the swiftness of incident. "13

    In his third book, Mid-American Chants (1918), Ander-
son abandoned the genre of the novel to explore in the more
intimate texture of poetry the inner realms of self. Though
Anderson's free-verse poems do not compare favorably with
the poetry of his best prose, they remain significant expressions of his inner life and reflect, perhaps, in their rhetorical rhythms and long, unrhymed lines the influence of Walt
Whitman. Important primarily for its insights into Anderson
the man, the collection nevertheless belongs to the author's
apprenticeship years and could not have served as a reliable
predictor of the power and talent displayed in Anderson's
fourth published work, Winesburg, Ohio.

    Winesburg is the story of "walls"--people walled in,
struggling to communicate, desperately attempting to reach
out and touch those around them, yet for the most part unable to crash the walls, unable to communicate meaningfully,
unable to escape their utter isolation. Each of the stories
focuses upon a character who has been twisted psychologically

into a spiritual grotesque.   The grotesques are warped, lonely individuals who are isolated because they are largely unable to transcend the intangible walls of self which imprison and stifle their attempts to love and understand others, while simultaneously preventing others from loving or understanding them.   Their loneliness and isolation are broken only in their communications with the young newspaper reporter, George Willard.

The grotesque see Willard as an instrument through which to tell their stories, a means of expressing the nature of the truths they live by, a way of transcending the walls which envelop them.   There is some evidence which indicates that Anderson intended for Willard to function in this way. Anderson, reflecting on the writing of Winesburg, recalls that at the time he was living in a small boarding house in Chicago, and that many of the Winesburg sketches resulted from his contact with fellow boarders.   He writes, "It was as though the people of that house, all of them wanting so much, none of them really equipped to wrestle with life as it was, had ... used me as an instrument.   They had got, I felt, through me, their stories told, and not in their own persons but, in a much more real and satisfactory way, through the lives of these queer small town people of the book. "[14]

In the stories of Winesburg, Anderson sensitively and honestly explores the problem of human isolation and loneliness.   Anderson realized that man is destined for the most part to live his life isolated within the walls of self.   He felt, "It may be life is only worth while at moments.   Perhaps, that is all we ought expect. "[15]   Those moments--captured best in the scene between George Willard and Helen White in "Sophistication"--consist of shattering the walls, seeing beneath the surface of reality, and knowing the quiet ecstasy of pure and total love and understanding.

Anderson, no doubt, attempted to write with high moral purpose of small town American life in the wake of an onrushing industrialism.   However, as he later wrote, the reception of Winesburg "amazed and confounded me.   The book was widely condemned, called nasty and dirty by most of its critics. "[16]   While many critics did respond negatively to what they perceived as an utterly stark view of life and a twisted concern with the pathological element of society, many others greeted Winesburg with enthusiasm, hailing its author as a short story innovator with daring insight and skill.   The book has since come to be seen as an American classic and has

received far more critical attention than any of Anderson's
other works.

In 1920, Anderson published his third novel, Poor
White, which again explores the effects of industrialism upon
the lives of people in a tiny midwestern community. While
the novel remains important for its historical dramatization
of the transition of the small town in America into the industrialized urban community, the book nevertheless is structurally flawed by interruptive digressions and an indecisive
conclusion.

In his next two books, The Triumph of the Egg (1921)
and Horses and Men (1923), Anderson returned to the short
story form with which he was always more comfortable and,
inevitably, more competent. In 1921, Anderson was awarded
the first Dial prize of two thousand dollars for The Triumph
of the Egg, which like Winesburg focuses upon the lives of
characters who have become grotesque. Unlike Winesburg,
however, Anderson's vision in The Triumph of the Egg is
deeply dark, suggesting a pathetic hopelessness in the lives
of the characters he creates. In Horses and Men Anderson
continues his attempt to understand the essential truths which
underlie the dark surface of life. Again his vision is dark
and uncertain, like hands reaching out into the night, seeking
to discover the form of truths concealed in blackness. Certain of the stories--"The Egg," "I Want To Know Why," and
"The Sad Horn-Blowers"--rank with the finest work in the entire Anderson canon.

In Many Marriages (1923), Anderson describes the attempt of John Webster, a washing-machine manufacturer, to
break away from traditional middle-class values and find personal truth and fulfillment. A grotesque spiritually akin to
many of the characters in Winesburg, Webster abandons his
wife and family to run off with his secretary, but at the end
of the novel still finds himself hopelessly trapped, unable to
realize fulfillment. Though marred by structural and character flaws common to nearly all Anderson's novels, Many
Marriages nevertheless "raises a prophetic and passionate
cry against the sloth of our hearts, the atrophy of our senses,
the cowardice of our thoughts."[17]

Dark Laughter (1925), the only one of Anderson's
novels to become a best-seller, contrasts the civilized laughter of a sterile white society with the natural "dark laughter"
of the Negro in the South. Profits from the book enabled

Anderson to build his beautiful home, Ripshin, near Marion,
Virginia.   Critics were more receptive to Dark Laughter than
to any of Anderson's previous novels, for as Herschel Brickell argues, "Anderson proves in Dark Laughter that he has
sufficient technical resources to encompass the writing of a
well integrated, skillfully done novel. "[18]   And Robert Morss
Lovett believed that in Dark Laughter more than in any earlier novel Anderson achieved "an artistic unity through a
clearer view and a stronger, more persistent grasp of his
material and meaning. "[19]

        In two semi-autobiographical works, A Story Teller's
Story (1924) and Tar: A Midwest Childhood (1926), Anderson
attempts to evaluate his own life and accomplishments against
the background of a changing American Midwest.   These were
followed by two collections of essays and sketches, Sherwood
Anderson's Notebook (1926) and A New Testament (1927), and
in 1929 by Hello Towns!, a collection of newspaper articles
organized to represent a year in the life of both Anderson
and the town where he lived, Marion, Virginia.

        Suffering from a lack of critical attention and the
charge that he had nothing new to say, Anderson published
Beyond Desire in 1932.   The book, which utilizes four interrelated novelettes as its central focus, reads like weak Marx-
ist fiction examining the New South and its socio-economic
complexities.   To critics, it established only further proof
of Anderson's weakness as a novelist.

        In 1936, Anderson published his final novel, Kit Bran-
don, which Roger Sergel has acclaimed as Anderson's "best
novel, and, by any standard, a great novel. "[20]   The novel
explores rumrunning in America's prohibition days as Anderson makes mountain girls, hillbillies, and moonshine integral-
ly appropriate to the demands of art.   Many critics, however, shared the sentiments of Mark Van Doren, who likened
Anderson more to a baby groping than to an artist writing
purposely with a story to tell.

        Sandwiched between Anderson's last two novels was
Death in the Woods (1933), a collection of stories that contains some of Anderson's finest fiction.   In stories like
"Death in the Woods" and "Brother Death" Anderson recap-
tured the power and perception of his earlier short-story collections.   Yet critics were generally insensitive to Anderson's achievement.   T. S. Mathews wrote that he was "so
used to Anderson now, to his puzzled confidences, his groping

repetitions, his occasional stumblings into real inspiration
that perhaps we tend to underrate him as an American phenomenon. Or perhaps we no longer overrate him. "21

    At the end of his life Anderson himself recognized
his status as a minor figure. However, few minor figures
have continued to demand the critical attention that has been
Anderson's since his death in 1941. Perhaps he continues to
receive attention because of the influence he exerted over a
generation of younger writers that included Faulkner, Hemingway, Farrell, and Wolfe. Certainly his influence has been
important. Nonetheless, I am inclined to believe that the current pinnacle of interest in Anderson derives from the intrin-
sic satisfaction that two generations have received from reading his fiction. The best of his work--the short story collections and parts of the novels--reveal a sensitive man attempting to explore life's inner realities with an honesty and
integrity that are beyond reproach. In the face of an overwhelming industrialism, Anderson asserts an element of hope
that human values can and will endure.

About This Book

    I have attempted to compile an efficient and useful bib-
liographic tool for students of Anderson. While fairly comprehensive, the bibliography is not exhaustive and focuses essentially upon English and American criticisms of Anderson.
Students wishing information on translations and foreign criticism should consult the bibliographic publishings of Dr. Ray
Lewis White (see entries 634 and 635).

    I have attempted to summarize critics' main argu-
ments in the annotations of this volume. Certain articles
are unannotated because they were unavailable to me at the
time of publication. I have chosen not to annotate book reviews and doctoral dissertations and have omitted master's
theses.

    My main objective has been to save students, scholars,
and teachers time, energy, and frustration in locating works
of Anderson and biographical-critical information about him.
Should this book achieve that objective, then my own expen-
diture of time and effort will have been worthwhile.

                              Douglas G. Rogers
                              University of Chicago
                              August 15, 1975

Notes

1. Irving Howe. SA: A Biographical and Critical Study (New York: William Sloan, 1951).

2. The most accurate depiction of Anderson's childhood remains William Sutton's excellent, but unfortunately unpublished doctoral dissertation, "SA: The Formative Years: 1876-1913," Ohio State University, 1943.

3. Sherwood Anderson. SA's Memoirs: A Critical Edition, ed. Ray Lewis White (Chapel Hill, North Carolina: University of North Carolina Press, 1969), p. 18.

4. Sherwood Anderson. "When I Left Business for Literature," Century, 107 (August 1924), p. 494.

5. For a detailed account of Anderson's departure from Elyria, see William A. Sutton, Exit to Elsinore (Muncie, Indiana: Ball State University Press, 1967).

6. Morris Wright. "Introduction," Windy McPherson's Son (Chicago: University of Chicago Press, 1965), p. ix.

7. Francis Hackett. "A New Novelist," Horizons (New York: Huebsch, 1918), p. 51.

8. Ibid., p. 55.

9. Waldo Frank. "Emerging Greatness," The Seven Arts, 1 (November 1916), p. 75.

10. Sherwood Anderson. Memoirs, ed. White, pp. 185-86.

11. Ibid., p. 186.

12. Francis Hackett. "To American Workingmen," Horizons (New York: Huebsch, 1918), p. 58.

13. Ibid., p. 58.

14. Sherwood Anderson. Memoirs, ed. White, p. 348.

15. Sherwood Anderson. Letters of SA, eds. Howard Mumford Jones and Walter B. Rideout (Boston: Little, Brown, and Company, 1953), p. 182.

16. Sherwood Anderson. SA's Memoirs, ed. Paul Rosen-
     feld (New York: Harcourt, Brace, and World, 1942),
     p. 294.

17. Ludwig Lewisohn. "Novelist and Prophet," Nation, 116
     (28 March 1923), p. 368.

18. Herschel Brickell. "An Armful of Fiction," Bookman,
     62 (November 1925), p. 338.

19. Robert Morss Lovett. "SA, American," Virginia Quar-
     terly Review, 17 (Summer 1941), p. 386.

20. Roger Sergel. "Of SA and Kit Brandon," Book Buyer,
     series r, v. 2, no. 7 (November 1936), p. 2.

21. T. S. Mathews. "Rather Bewildered," Commonweal,
     25 (20 November 1936), p. 110.

ACKNOWLEDGMENTS

In compiling a work of this type, one enters the debt of many individuals and institutions. I have had access to the following excellent libraries, and I wish to thank their highly professional and capable staffs: Newberry Library, University of Chicago Regenstein Library, Loyola University of Chicago Library, University of Colorado Library, and Colorado State University Library. A number of colleagues were extremely helpful in offering advice and information. I would especially thank Dr. David D. Anderson of Michigan State University, Dr. Hamlin Hill, Dr. Sheldon Sacks, and Mr. Richard Vine of the University of Chicago. Earlier bibliographers greatly assisted me in my research. I am most grateful to Eugene P. Sheehy, Kenneth A. Lohf, Ray Lewis White, Raymond D. Gozzi, Richard C. Johnson, and G. Thomas Tanselle for their collective contributions to Anderson scholarship. My greatest debt of thanks rests with Sally Rogers who volunteered long hours of typing, editing, and proofreading. Without her able assistance this book would have been months late in going to press.

D. G. R.

CHRONOLOGY

1876   September 13: born the third of seven children to Irvin and Emma Anderson in Camden, Ohio.

1884   Family settles in Clyde, Ohio, a town which later serves as semi-prototype for Winesburg.

1895   Serves in Company I, 16th Infantry of the Ohio National Guard. Anderson's mother, Emma, dies of consumption.

1896   Leaves Clyde to work in an apple warehouse in Chicago.

1898   Serves in Company I, Sixth Ohio Regiment of Volunteer Infantry, during Spanish-American War.

1900   June: graduates from Wittenberg Academy, Springfield, Ohio. Returns to Chicago; writes and sells advertising copy for the Crowell Publishing Company.

1904   May 16: marries Cornelia Lane in Toledo, Ohio.

1906   Assumes presidency of the United Factories Company in Cleveland, Ohio.

1907   August 16: first son, Robert, born. Starts a mail-order paint firm in Elyria, Ohio.

1908   The successful Anderson Manufacturing Company begins producing its own paint. December 31: second son, John, born.

1911   October 29: daughter, Marion born.

1912   Writes early drafts of Windy McPherson's Son and Marching Men. December 1: found dazed and suf-

14

fering from nervous exhaustion in Cleveland, Ohio.

1913   Leaves presidency of Anderson Manufacturing Com-
        pany; returns to work for Taylor-Critchfield Adver-
        tising Company in Chicago.

1914   July: first short story, "The Rabbit-Pen."

1915   Divorces Cornelia Lane. December: "Sister" ap-
        pears in Little Review.

1916   Windy McPherson's Son, first novel. Several of
        the Winesburg tales published: "The Book of the
        Grotesque," "Hands," and "The Strength of God"
        in Masses; "Paper Pills" in Little Review; "Queer"
        in The Seven Arts. Marries Tennessee Mitchell.

1917   Marching Men. Three Winesburg tales published:
        "The Untold Lie," "Mother," and "The Thinker" in
        The Seven Arts.

1918   Mid-American Chants. Two Winesburg tales pub-
        lished: "The Man of Ideas" and "An Awakening"
        in Little Review.

1919   Winesburg, Ohio.

1920   Poor White. Irwin Anderson, Sherwood's father,
        dies.

1921   The Triumph of the Egg. Wins Dial Award of two
        thousand dollars.

1923   Many Marriages. Horses and Men.

1924   A Story Teller's Story. Divorces Tennessee
        Mitchell. Marries Elizabeth Prall.

1925   The Modern Writer. Dark Laughter.

1926   Sherwood Anderson's Notebook. Tar: A Midwest
        Childhood. Purchases Ripshin Farm in Troutdale,
        Virginia.

1927   A New Testament. Buys two Marion, Virginia,
        newspapers: Smyth County News and Marion Demo-
        crat.

1929   Alice and the Lost Novel. Hello Towns! Nearer
        the Grass Roots. Separates from Elizabeth Prall.

1930   The American County Fair.

1931   Perhaps Women.

1932   Beyond Desire. Divorces Elizabeth Prall. Attends
        "World's Congress Against War" in Amsterdam.

1933   Death in the Woods and Other Stories. July: Mar-
        ries Eleanor Copenhaven.

1934   No Swank. First dramatic presentation of Wines-
        burg, Ohio at the Hedgerow Theatre.

1935   Puzzled America.

1936   Kit Brandon.

1937   Plays: Winesburg and Others (Includes three one-
        act plays: The Triumph of the Egg, Mother, and
        They Married Later).

1939   A Writer's Conception of Realism, the text of an
        address delivered on January 20, 1939, at Olivet
        College in Olivet, Michigan. Five Poems.

1940   Home Town.

1941   March 8: dies of peritonitis in colon, Panama
        Canal Zone, while engaged in a State Department-
        promoted goodwill tour of South America.

1942   Sherwood Anderson's Memoirs.

1969   Sherwood Anderson's Memoirs: A Critical Edition,
        edited by Ray Lewis White.

PART I

PRIMARY MATERIALS

A. INDIVIDUAL WORKS

1. Alice and the Lost Novel. London: Elkin Mathews and Marot, 1929.

2. The American County Fair. New York: Random House, 1930.

3. Beyond Desire. New York: Liveright, 1932.

4. Dark Laughter. New York: Boni and Liveright, 1925. London: Jarrolds, 1926.

5. Death in the Woods and Other Stories. New York: Liveright, 1933.

6. Five Poems. San Mateo, California: Quercus Press, 1939.

7. Hello Towns! New York: Horace Liveright, 1929.

8. Home Town. New York: Alliance Book Corporation, 1940.

9. Horses and Men: Tales, Long and Short, from Our American Life. New York: B. W. Huebsch, 1923.

10. Kit Brandon, A Portrait. New York: Charles Scribner's Sons, 1936.

11. Many Marriages. New York: B. W. Huebsch, 1923.

12. Marching Men. New York: John Lane, 1917. London: John Lane, 1917.

13. Mid-American Chants. New York: John Lane, 1918. London: John Lane, 1918.

14. The Modern Writer. San Francisco: Lantern Press, 1925.

19

15. Nearer the Grass Roots. San Francisco: Westgate
    Press, 1929.

16. A New Testament. New York: Boni and Liveright,
    1927.

17. No Swank. Philadelphia: Centaur Press, 1934.

18. Perhaps Women. New York: Horace Liveright, 1931.

19. Plays: Winesburg and Others. New York: Charles
    Scribner's Sons, 1937.

20. Poor White. New York: B. W. Huebsch, 1920. Lon-
    don: Jonathan Cape, 1921.

21. Puzzled America. New York: Charles Scribner's
    Sons, 1935.

22. Sherwood Anderson's Memoirs. (Edited by Paul Rosen-
    feld) New York: Harcourt, Brace and World, 1942.

23. Sherwood Anderson's Notebook. New York: Boni and
    Liveright, 1926.

24. A Story Teller's Story. New York: B. W. Huebsch,
    1924. London: Jonathan Cape, 1925.

25. Tar: A Midwest Childhood. New York: Boni and
    Liveright, 1926. London: Martin Secker, 1927.

26. The Triumph of the Egg. New York: B. W. Huebsch,
    1921.

27. Windy McPherson's Son. New York: John Lane, 1916.
    London, John Lane, 1916.

28. Winesburg, Ohio. New York: B. W. Huebsch, 1919.
    London: Jonathan Cape, 1922.

    B.   EDITIONS, COLLECTIONS, AND REPRINTS

29. Alice and the Lost Novel. Belfast, Maine: Porter, 1971.

30. Alice and the Lost Novel. Folcroft, Pennsylvania: Folcroft, 1971.

31. Beyond Desire. New York: Liveright, 1961.

32. Buck Fever Papers. Welford D. Taylor, ed. Charlottesville, Virginia: University Press of Virginia, 1971.

33. Dark Laughter. New York: Liveright, 1960.

34. Dark Laughter. New York: Liveright, 1970.

35. Hello Towns! Mamaroneck, New York: Paul P. Appel, 1970.

36. Homage to SA. Paul P. Appel, ed. Mamaroneck, New York: Paul P. Appel, 1970.

37. Marching Men. Ray Lewis White, ed. Cleveland: Press of Case Western Reserve University, 1972.

38. Mid-American Chants. Berkeley: Frontier Press, 1972.

39. No Swank. Mamaroneck, New York: Paul P. Appel, 1970.

40. Perhaps Women. Mamaroneck, New York: Paul P. Appel, 1970.

41. Poor White. New York: Modern Library, 1926.

42. Poor White. New York: Viking Press, 1966.

43. The Portable SA. Horace Gregory, ed. New York: Viking Press, 1949; rev. ed. New York: Viking Press, 1972.

44. Puzzled America. Mamaroneck, New York: Paul P. Appel, 1970.

45. Return to Winesburg: Selections from Four Years of Writing for a Country Newspaper. Ray Lewis White, ed. Chapel Hill: University of North Carolina Press, 1967.

46. Selected Short Stories of SA. Edition for the Armed

Services, Inc., 1945.

47. The Sherwood Anderson Reader. Paul Rosenfeld, ed.
     Boston: Houghton Mifflin, 1947.

48. SA: Short Stories. Maxwell Geismar, ed. New York:
     Hill and Wang, 1962.

49. SA's Memoirs: A Critical Edition. Ray Lewis White,
     ed. Chapel Hill: University of North Carolina Press,
     1969.

50. SA's Notebook. Mamaroneck, New York: Paul P. Ap-
     pel, 1970.

51. A Story Teller's Story. New York: Viking Press,
     1969.

52. A Story Teller's Story: A Critical Text. Ray Lewis
     White, ed. Cleveland: Press of Case Western Re-
     serve University, 1968.

53. Tar: A Midwest Childhood: A Critical Text. Ray
     Lewis White, ed. Cleveland: Press of Case Western
     Reserve University, 1969.

54. Windy McPherson's Son. Rev. ed. New York: B. W.
     Huebsch, 1921.

55. Windy McPherson's Son. Chicago: University of Chi-
     cago Press, 1965.

56. Winesburg, Ohio. New York: Modern Library, 1922.

57. Winesburg, Ohio. New York: Viking Press, 1960.

58. Winesburg, Ohio: Text and Criticism. John H. Fer-
     res, ed. New York: Viking Press, 1966.

59. The Writer's Book: A Critical Edition. Martha Mul-
     roy Curry, ed. Metuchen, New Jersey: Scarecrow
     Press, 1975.

Note: two significant volumes scheduled for 1975-76 publications are listed below:

60. Dear Bab: Letters of SA to a Friend. William A.

Sutton, ed. DeLand, Florida: Everett/Edwards, 1975.
The volume will include 308 letters to Marietta D. Fin-
ley Hahn of Indianapolis, written between September,
1916, and March, 1933. Mrs. Hahn, the M.D.F. who
shared the dedication of Sherwood Anderson's Notebook
with John Emerson, was a very close friend who took
great interest in Anderson's work and rendered him
considerable financial aid.

61. Untitled Commemorative Volume on SA. Hilbert H.
Campbell and Charles E. Modlin, eds. Troy, New
York: Whitston, 1976. A supplementary volume to
the September, 1976 issue of American Notes and
Queries, the book will include an inventory of Anderson's library, some previously unpublished letters, and
biographical and critical articles on SA.

C. ARTICLES AND STORIES

62. "Aching Breasts and Snow-White Hearts." Vanity
Fair, 25 (January 1926), pp. 51, 108.

63. "Adventures in Form and Color." Little Review, 7
(January-March 1921), p. 64.

64. "Advertising a Nation." Agricultural Advertising, 12
(May 1905), p. 389.

65. "Alfred Steiglitz." New Republic, 32 (25 October
1922), pp. 215-17.

66. "America on a Cultural Jag." Saturday Review of
Literature, 4 (3 December 1927), pp. 364-65.

67. "American Spectator." American Spectator, 2, no. 16
(February 1934), p. 1.

68. "Another Wife." Scribner's Magazine, 80 (December
1926), pp. 587-94.

69. "An Apology for Crudity." Dial, 63 (8 November 1917),
pp. 437-38.

70.   "An Awakening." Little Review, 5 (December 1918),
      pp. 13-21.

71.   "At Amsterdam." New Masses, 8 (November 1932),
      p. 11.

72.   "At the Nine Mouth." Today, 1 (30 December 1933),
      pp. 5, 19-21.

73.   "Backstage with a Martyr." Coronet, 8 (July 1940),
      pp. 39-41.

74.   "Beauty." Harper's Bazaar, 63 (January 1929), pp.
      78-79, 118.

75.   "Betrayed." Golden Book, 1 (May 1925), pp. 743-44.

76.   "Blackfoot's Masterpiece." Forum, 55 (June 1916),
      pp. 679-83.

77.   "Blue Smoke." Today, 1 (24 February 1934), pp. 6-
      7, 23.

78.   "Boardwalk Fireworks." Today, 5 (9 November 1935),
      pp. 6-7, 19.

79.   "Broken." Century, 105 (March 1923), pp. 643-56.

80.   "Brothers." Bookman, 53 (April 1921), pp. 110-15.

81.   "Brown Boomer." Signatures, 3 (Winter 1937-38), pp.
      302-08.

82.   "Burt Emmett." Colophon, 1 (Summer 1935), pp. 7-9.

83.   "A Businessman's Reading." Reader, 2 (October
      1903), pp. 503-04.

84.   "Business Types: The Boyish Man." Agricultural Ad-
      vertising, 11 (October 1904), p. 53.

85.   "Business Types: The Discouraged Man." Agricul-
      tural Advertising, 11 (July 1904), pp. 43-44.

86.   "Business Types: The Good Fellow." Agricultural
      Advertising, 11 (January 1904), p. 36.

87. "Business Types: The Hot Young'un and the Cold Old'un." Agricultural Advertising, 11 (September 1904), pp. 24-26.

88. "Business Types: The Liar--A Vacation Story." Agricultural Advertising, 11 (June 1904), pp. 27-29.

89. "Business Types: The Man of Affairs." Agricultural Advertising, 11 (March 1904), pp. 36-38.

90. "Business Types: Silent Men." Agricultural Advertising, 11 (February 1904), p. 19.

91. "Business Types: The Solicitor." Agricultural Advertising, 11 (August 1904), pp. 21-24.

92. "Business Types: The Traveling Man." Agricultural Advertising, 11 (April 1904), pp. 39-40.

93. "Business Types: The Undeveloped Man." Agricultural Advertising, 11 (May 1904), pp. 31-32.

94. "Carl Sandburg." Bookman, 54 (December 1921), pp. 360-61.

95. "Caught." American Mercury, 1 (February 1924), pp. 165-76.

96. "Censorship." Laughing Horse, 17 (February 1930), p. 5.

97. "Chicago--A Feeling." Vanity Fair, 27 (October 1926), pp. 53, 118.

98. "City Gangs Enslave Moonshine Mountaineers." Liberty, 12 (2 November 1935), pp. 12-13.

99. "Cityscapes." American Spectator, 2, no. 16 (February 1934), p. 2.

100. "Communications." American Spectator, 1, no. 11 (September 1933), p. 2.

100a. "A Complete Handbook of Opinion." Vanity Fair, 30 (April 1928), pp. 68-69.

101. "Confessions and Letters: Questionnaire." Little Re-

view, 12 (May 1929), pp. 12-13.

102. "The Contract." Broom, 1 (December 1921), pp. 148-53.

103. "The Corn Planting." American Magazine, 118 (November 1934), pp. 47, 149-50; Penguine Parade, 1 (November 1937), pp. 115-22.

104. "Cotton Mill." Scribner's Magazine, 88 (July 1930), pp. 1-11.

105. "Country Town Notes." Vanity Fair, 32 (May 1929), pp. 112, 126.

106. "The Country Weekly." Forum, 85 (April 1931), pp. 208-13.

107. "County Squires." Vanity Fair, 33 (October 1929), pp. 63, 128.

108. "A Criminal's Christmas." Vanity Fair, 27 (December 1926), pp. 89, 130.

109. "The Cry in the Night." Vanity Fair, 37 (September 1931), pp. 49-50.

110. "The Dance Is On." The Rotarian, 58 (June 1941), p. 7.

111. "Danville, Virginia." New Republic, 65 (21 January 1931), pp. 266-68.

112. "A Dead Dog." Yale Review, 20 (Spring 1931), pp. 554-67.

113. "Death in the Woods." American Mercury, 9 (September 1926), pp. 7-13.

114. "Delegation." New Yorker, 9 (9 December 1933), pp. 36, 38.

115. "Desperate Need." Nation, 135 (23 November 1932), p. 506.

116. "Discovery of a Father." Reader's Digest, 35 (November 1939), pp. 21-25.

117. "Domestic and Juvenile." Vanity Fair, 34 (March 1939), pp. 35-37.

118. "The Door of the Trap." Dial, 68 (May 1920), pp. 567-76.

119. "Dreiser." Little Review, 3 (April 1916), p. 5.

120. "Educating an Author." Vanity Fair, 28 (May 1927), pp. 47-48.

121. "Elizabethon, Tennessee." Nation, 128 (1 May 1929), pp. 526-27.

122. "An Estimate of 'Mr. and Mrs. Philip Wase.'" Vanity Fair, 25 (November 1925), pp. 57, 94.

123. "Explain! Explain! Again Explain!" Today, 1 (2 December 1933), p. 3.

124. "Factory Town." New Republic, 62 (26 March 1930), pp. 143-44.

125. "The Far West." Vanity Fair, 27 (January 1927), pp. 39-40.

126. "The Farmer Wears Clothes." Agricultural Advertising, 9 (February 1902), p. 6.

127. "Feud." American Magazine, 119 (February 1935), pp. 71, 112-14.

128. "The Fight." Vanity Fair, 29 (October 1927), pp. 72, 106, 108.

129. "Five Poems." American Mercury, 11 (May 1927), pp. 26-27.

130. "For What?" Yale Review, 30 (June 1941), pp. 750-58.

131. "Four American Impressions." New Republic, 32 (11 October 1922), pp. 171-73.

132. "From Chicago." Seven Arts, 2 (May 1917), pp. 41-9.

133. "From Little Things." This Week (11 February 1940),
      p. 2.

134. "The Fussy Man and the Trimmer." Agricultural Ad-
      vertising, 11 (December 1904), pp. 79-82.

135. "Gertrude Stein." American Spectator, 2, No. 18
      (April 1934), p. 3.

136. "Gertrude Stein's Kitchen." Wings, 7, No. 9 (Sep-
      tember 1933), pp. 12-13, 26.

137. "A Ghost Story." Vanity Fair, 29 (December 1927),
      pp. 78-142.

138. "Girl By the Stove." Decision, 1 (January 1941), pp.
      19-22.

139. "Give a Child Room to Grow." Parent's Magazine,
      11 (April 1936), p. 17.

140. "Give Rex Tugwell a Chance." Today, 4 (8 June
      1935), pp. 5, 21.

141. "The Good Life at Hedgerow." Esquire, 6 (October
      1936), pp. 51, 198A, 198B, 199.

142. "A Good One." New Republic, 85 (8 January 1936),
      p. 259.

143. "A Great Factory." Vanity Fair, 27 (November 1926),
      pp. 51-52.

144. "Hands." Masses, 8 (March 1916), pp. 5, 7.

145. "Hard Boiled." Direction, 1, No. 4 (April 1938),
      pp. 8-9.

146. "Hello, Big Boy." Vanity Fair, 26 (July 1926), pp.
      41-42, 88.

147. "Hello Yank." Saturday Review, 132 (6 August 1921),
      pp. 172-74; Living Age, 311 (15 October 1921), pp.
      173-75.

148. "Here They Come." Esquire, 13 (March 1940), pp.
      80-81.

149. "His Chest of Drawers." Household Magazine, 39
      (August 1939), pp. 4-5.

150. "How I Came to Communism: Symposium." New
      Masses, 8 (September 1932), pp. 8-9.

151. "I Get So I Can't Go On." Story, 3 (December 1933),
      pp. 55-62.

152. "I Live a Dozen Lives." American Magazine, 128
      (October 1939), p. 58.

153. "I Want to Know Why." Smart Set, 60 (November
      1919), pp. 35-40.

154. "I Want to Work." Today, 1 (28 April 1934), pp.
      11-12, 22.

155. "I Was a Bad Boy." This Week (18 May 1941), pp.
      12, 17.

156. "I Will Not Sell My Papers." Outlook, 150 (5 Decem-
      ber 1928), pp. 1286-87.

157. "I'm a Fool." Dial, 72 (February 1922), pp. 119-29.

158. "An Impression of Mexico--Its People." Southern
      Literary Messenger, 1 (April 1939), pp. 241-42.

159. "In a Boxcar." Vanity Fair, 31 (October 1928), pp.
      76, 114.

160. "In a Strange Town." Scribner's Magazine, 87 (Janu-
      ary 1930), pp. 20-25.

161. "Italian Poet in America." Decision, 2 (August 1941),
      pp. 8-15.

162. "It's a Woman's Age." Scribner's Magazine, 88 (De-
      cember 1930), pp. 613-18.

163. "J. J. Lankes and His Woodcuts." Virginia Quarterly
      Review, 7 (January 1931), pp. 18-27.

164. "Jug of Moon." Today, 2 (15 September 1934), pp.
      6-7, 23.

165. "A Jury Case." American Mercury, 12 (December 1927), pp. 431-34.

166. "Just Walking." Vanity Fair, 30 (April 1928), pp. 76, 108.

167. "A Landed Proprietor." The Rotarian, 58 (March 1941), pp. 8-10.

168. "Legacies of Ford Madox Ford." Coronet, 8 (August 1940), pp. 135-36.

169. "Let's Go Somewhere." Outlook, 151 (13 February 1929), pp. 247, 278, 280.

170. "Let's Have More Criminal Syndicalism." New Masses, 7 (February 1932), pp. 3-6.

171. [Letter to the Editor.] Bookman, 75 (October 1932), p. 564.

172. "Letters to Van Wyck Brooks." Story, 19 (September-October 1941), pp. 19-62.

173. "Lift Up Thine Eyes." Nation, 130 (28 May 1930), pp. 620-22.

174. "Lindsay and Masters." New Republic, 85 (25 December 1935), pp. 194-95.

175. "The Line-Up." American Spectator, 2, No. 20 (June 1934), p. 1.

176. "Listen, Hollywood!" Photoplay, 52 (March 1938), pp. 28-29.

177. "Listen, Mr. President." Nation, 135 (31 August 1932), pp. 191-93.

178. "Little Magazines." Intermountain Review, 2, No. 2 (Fall 1937), p. 1.

179. "Little People and Big Words." Reader's Digest, 39 (September 1941), pp. 118-20.

180. "A Living Force in Literature." Brentano's Book Chat (June 1921), pp. 17-18.

181. "Living in America." Nation, 120 (10 June 1925), pp. 657-58.

182. "Look Out, Brown Man!" Nation, 131 (26 November 1930), pp. 579-80.

183. "Loom Dance." New Republic, 62 (30 April 1930), pp. 292-94.

184. "The Lost Novel." Scribner's Magazine, 84 (September 1928), 255-58.

185. "Machine Child-Rearing." New York Times (8 November 1931), p. 2.

186. "Machine Song: Automobile." Household Magazine, 30 (October 1930), p. 3.

187. "The Magnificent Idler." Reader's Digest, 28 (February 1936), pp. 88-90.

188. "Making it Clear." Agricultural Advertising, 24 (February 1913), p. 16.

189. "The Man and the Book." Reader, 3 (December 1903), pp. 71-73.

190. "The Man at the Filling Station." Vanity Fair, 30 (August 1928), pp. 53, 88, 90.

191. "The Man in the Brown Coat." Little Review, 7 (January-March 1921), pp. 18-21.

192. "A Man's Mind." New Republic, 63 (21 May 1930), pp. 22-23.

193. "A Man's Song of Life." Virginia Quarterly Review, 9 (January 1933), pp. 108-14.

194. "The Man's Story." Dial, 75 (September 1923), pp. 247-64.

195. "Many Marriages." Dial, 73 (October 1922), pp. 361-82; 73 (November 1922), pp. 533-48; 73 (December 1922), 623-44; 74 (January 1923), pp. 31-49; 74 (February 1923), pp. 165-82; 74 (March 1923), pp. 256-72.

196. "Maury Maverick in San Antonio." New Republic,
      102 (25 March 1940), pp. 398-400.

197. "Meeting Ring Lardner." New Yorker, 9 (25 Novem-
      ber 1933), pp. 36, 38.

198. "A Meeting South." Dial, 78 (April 1925), pp. 269-
      79.

199. "Mid-American Prayer." Seven Arts, 2 (June 1917),
      pp. 190-92.

200. "Mid-American Songs." Poetry, 10 (September 1917),
      pp. 281-91.

201. "Mill Girls." Scribner's Magazine, 91 (January 1932),
      pp. 8-12, 59-64.

202. "Mr. Joe's Doctor." American Magazine, 118 (Au-
      gust 1934), pp. 81-82.

203. "A Moonlight Walk." Red Book, 70 (December 1937),
      pp. 43-45, 100-04.

204. "Mother." Seven Arts, 1 (March 1917), pp. 452-61.

205. "Motor Trip." American Spectator, 2, No. 22 (Au-
      gust 1934), p. 9.

206. "A Mountain Dance." Vanity Fair, 29 (November
      1927), pp. 59, 110.

207. "A Mountain Marriage." Fight Against War and
      Fascism, 3 (October 1936), pp. 16-17, 25.

208. "My Fire Burns." Survey, 47 (25 March 1922), pp.
      997-1000.

209. "The Nationalist." American Spectator, 2, No. 14
      (December 1933), p. 1; Fortnightly Review, 142 (July
      1934), pp. 24-29; American Spectator Yearbook. New
      York: F. A. Stokes, 1934, pp. 3-10.

210. "Nearer the Grass Roots." Outlook, 148 (January
      1928), pp. 3-4, 27.

211. "A New Chance for the Men of the Hills." Today,
      1 (12 May 1934), pp. 10-11, 22-23.

212.   "The New Englander." Dial, 70 (February 1921),
       pp. 143-58.

213.   "The New Note." Little Review, 1 (March 1914), p.
       23.

214.   "New Orleans: A Prose Poem in the Expressionist
       Manner." Vanity Fair, 26 (August 1926), pp. 36, 97.

215.   "New Orleans, The Double Dealer and the Modern
       Movement in America." Double Dealer, 3 (March
       1922), pp. 119-26.

216.   "New Paths for Old." Today, 1 (7 April 1934), pp.
       12-13, 32.

217.   "A New Testament." Double Dealer, 3 (February
       1922), pp. 64-67.

218.   "A New Testament (The Visit in the Morning; Negro
       on the Docks; The Ripper; Chicago; Hunger; Death)."
       Vanity Fair, 28 (April 1927), p. 75.

219.   "A New Testament: The Builder." Double Dealer,
       3 (June 1922), p. 311.

220.   "A New Testament: A Man Speaks out of the New
       Confusion." Playboy, 2 No. 1 (First Quarter 1923),
       pp. 9-11.

221.   "A New Testament: Testament One." Little Review,
       6 (October 1919), pp. 3-6.

221a. "A New Testament: Testament Two." Little Review,
       6 (November 1919), pp. 19-21.

222.   "A New Testament: III." Little Review, 6 (Decem-
       ber 1919), pp. 17-19.

223.   "A New Testament: IV-V." Little Review, 6 (Janu-
       ary 1920), pp. 15-17.

224.   "A New Testament, VI-IX." Little Review, 6 (March
       1920), pp. 12-16.

225.   "A New Testament: X." Little Review, 6 (April
       1920), pp. 58-60.

226. "A New Testament: XI-XII." Little Review, 7
     (July-August 1920), pp. 58-61.

227. "A New Testament: XIII." Double Dealer, 6 (Au-
     gust-September 1924), pp. 181-82.

228. "New Tyrants of the Land." Today, 1 (26 May 1934),
     pp. 10-11, 20.

229. "New York." Vanity Fair, 28 (July 1927), pp. 33, 94.

230. "Nice Girl." New Yorker, 12 (25 July 1936), pp.
     15-17.

231. "No Swank." Today, 1 (11 November 1933), pp. 4-5,
     23-24.

232. "Nobody's Home." Today, 3 (30 March 1935), pp.
     6-7, 20-21.

233. "Northwest Unafraid." Today, 3 (12 January 1935),
     pp. 8-9, 22-23.

234. "Not Knocking." Agricultural Advertising, 9 (Decem-
     ber 1902), pp. 22-23.

235. "Not Sixteen." Tomorrow, 5 (March 1946), pp. 28-
     32.

236. "A Note on Realism." New York Evening Post
     Literary Review (25 October 1924), pp. 1-2.

237. "A Note on Story Tellers." Vanity Fair, 28 (August
     1927), pp. 42, 82.

238. "Notes Out of a Man's Life." Vanity Fair, 26 (March
     1926), pp. 47, 98.

239. "The Novelist." Little Review, 2 (January-February
     1916), pp. 12-14.

240. "Off Balance." New Yorker, 9 (5 August 1933), pp.
     12-14.

241. "Oh, the Big Words!" This Week (31 March 1940),
     p. 2.

242. "Ohio: I'll Say We've Done Well." Nation, 115 (9 August 1922), pp. 146-48.

243. "On Being a Country Editor." Vanity Fair, 29 (February 1928), 70, 92.

244. "On Being Published." Colophon (February 1930).

245. "On Conversing with Authors." Vanity Fair, 28 (June 1927), pp. 40, 98.

246. "The Other Woman." Little Review, 7 (May-June 1920), pp. 37-44.

247. "Out of Nowhere into Nothing." Dial, 71 (July 1921), pp. 1-18; (August 1921), pp. 153-69; (September 1921), pp. 325-46.

248. "Pages from a New Testament." Vanity Fair, 19 (October 1922), p. 57.

249. "Pastoral." Red Book, 74 (January 1940), pp. 38-39, 59.

250. "Paying for Old Sins." Nation, 139 (11 July 1934), pp. 49-50.

251. "The Persistent Liar." Tomorrow, 6 (September 1946), pp. 10-12.

252. "Personal Protest." Canadian Forum, 17 (August 1937), pp. 168-69.

253. "The Philosopher." Little Review, 3 (June-July 1916), pp. 7-9.

254. "A Plan." Modern Monthly, 7 (February 1933), pp. 13-16.

255. "Pop." New Yorker, 9 (27 May 1933), p. 12.

256. "Price of Aristocracy." Today, 1 (10 March 1934), pp. 10-11.

257. "Prohibition." Vanity Fair, 27 (February 1927), pp. 68, 96.

258.   "Queer." Seven Arts, 1 (December 1916), pp. 97-
       108.

259.   "Questionnaire." Little Review, 12 (May 1929), pp.
       12-13.

260.   "The Rabbit-pen." Harper's, 129 (July 1914), pp.
       207-19.

261.   "Real-Unreal." New Republic, 63 (11 June 1930),
       pp. 103-04.

262.   "The Return." Century, 110 (May 1925), pp. 3-14.

263.   "The Right to Die: Dinner in Thessaly." Forum,
       95 (January 1936), pp. 40-41.

264.   "A Robin's Egg Renaissance." Story, 19 (September-
       October 1941), pp. 11-48.

265.   "Rot and Reason." Agricultural Advertising, 10 (No-
       vember 1903), pp. 56-58. (About Stunts; About In-
       quiries; About Cleverness; About Suspicion; Para-
       graphs.)

266.   "Rot and Reason." Agricultural Advertising, 10
       (April 1903), pp. 12-14. (Doing Stunts; Packingham;
       Of No Value; Chicago Inspirations; The Stamp as a
       Salesman.)

267.   "Rot and Reason." Agricultural Advertising, 10 (Au-
       gust 1903), pp. 22-25. (The Golden Harvest Farmer;
       Golden Harvest Manufacturers; The Golden Fake.)

268.   "Rot and Reason." Agricultural Advertising, 10
       (June 1903), pp. 54-57. (Knock No. 1; Knock No. 2;
       Boast No. 1.)

269.   "Rot and Reason." Agricultural Advertising, 10
       (March 1903), pp. 18-20. (The Lightweight; The
       Born Quitter.)

270.   "Rot and Reason." Agricultural Advertising, 10
       (February 1903), pp. 13-16. (The New Job; The
       Laugh of Scorn; The Traveling Man; Push, Push,
       Push; Unfinished Contracts.)

271. "Rot and Reason." Agricultural Advertising, 10 (July 1903), pp. 22-26. (Office Tone; Fun and Work; Work in the Dark.)

272. "Rot and Reason." Agricultural Advertising, 10 (December 1903), pp. 50-51. (The Old and the New; A Christmas Thought; Men that are Wanted.)

273. "Rot and Reason." Agricultural Advertising, 10 (October 1903), pp. 17-19. (Twenty Years in the West; What Henry George Said Twenty Years Ago; Twenty Years in Figures; Fairs.)

274. "Rot and Reason." Agricultural Advertising, 10 (May 1903), pp. 20-22. (Unfinished; Finding Our Work.)

275. "The Sad Horn Blowers." Harper's, 146 (February 1923), pp. 273-89.

276. "The Sales Master and the Selling Corporation." Agricultural Advertising, 12 (April 1905), pp. 306-08.

277. "Samovar." American Spectator, 2, No. 21 (July 1934), p. 3.

278. "Seeds." Little Review, 5 (July 1918), pp. 24-31; English Review, 34 (January 1922), pp. 13-20.

279. "Senility." Little Review, 5, (September 1918), pp. 37-39.

280. "A Sentimental Journey." Vanity Fair, 29 (January 1928), pp. 46, 118.

281. "SA Goes Home." Today, 3 (8 December 1934), pp. 6-7, 23.

282. "SA to Theodore Dreiser." American Spectator, 1, No. 8 (June 1933), p. 1.

283. "Sister." Little Review, 2 (December 1915), pp. 3-4.

284. "Sit-downers Stick: Opinions." Literary Digest, 123 (13 February 1937), p. 8.

285. "The Situation in American Writing: Seven Questions (Part II)." Partisan Review, 6, No. 5 (Fall 1939), pp. 103-05.

286. "A Small Boy Looks at His World." Woman's Home
      Companion, 53 (July 1926), pp. 19-20, 42, 45.

287. "Small Town Notes." Vanity Fair, 30 (June 1928),
      pp. 58, 120; 32 (April 1929), pp. 72, 106; 32 (July
      1929), pp. 48, 110; 33 (September 1929), pp. 72, 110,
      114.

288. "So You Want to Be a Writer?" Saturday Review of
      Literature, 21 (9 December 1939), pp. 13-14. Con-
      densed version in Reader's Digest, 36 (January 1940),
      pp. 109-11.

289. "'Sold!' To the American Tobacco Company." Globe,
      2 (July 1938), pp. 30-35; condensed version in Youth
      Today, 2 (September 1939), pp. 28-30.

290. "A Soliloquy." Agricultural Advertising, 9 (April
      1902), p. 25.

291. "The South." Vanity Fair, 27 (September 1926), pp.
      49-50, 138.

292. "Statements of Belief II; Further Credos of America's
      Leading Authors." Bookman, 68 (October 1928), p.
      204.

293. "Stewart's on the Square." New Yorker, 10 (9 June
      1934), pp. 77-80.

294. "Stolen Day." This Week (27 April 1941), pp. 6, 23.

295. "The Story Teller's Job." Book Buyer, 2, No. 8
      (December 1936), p. 8.

296. "A Story-teller's Story." Phantasmus, 1 (May-June
      1924), pp. 1-37, 109-64.

297. "The Story Writers." Smart Set, 48 (January 1916),
      pp. 243-48.

298. "The Strength of God." Masses, 8 (August 1916), pp.
      12-13.

299. "The Struggle." Little Review, 3 (May 1916), pp.
      7-10.

300. "Tar Moorhead's Father." Woman's Home Companion, 53 (June 1926), pp. 19-20, 154-55.

301. "Tar's Day of Bravery." Woman's Home Companion, 53 (October 1926), pp. 25-26, 184-85.

302. "Tar's Wonderful Sunday." Woman's Home Companion, 53 (November 1926), pp. 29-30, 50.

303. "Testament (Containing Songs of One Who Would Be a Priest); Song Number Two." Double Dealer, 7 (November-December 1924), pp. 59-60.

304. "Testament: One Puzzled Concerning Himself." Double Dealer, 7 (January-February 1925), p. 100.

305. "Testament: Song Number One." Double Dealer, 7 (October 1924), pp. 15-16.

306. "Testament of Two Glad Men." Double Dealer, 3 (April 1922), pp. 203-05.

307. "These Mountaineers." Vanity Fair, 33 (January 1930), pp. 44-45, 94.

308. "They Come Bearing Gifts." American Mercury, 21 (October 1930), pp. 129-37.

309. "They Got This One." Book Buyer, 1, No. 4 (June 1935), pp. 10-11.

310. "The Thinker." Seven Arts, 2 (September 1917), pp. 584-97.

311. "To Remember." American Spectator, 1, No. 7 (May 1933), p. 1. Reprinted in American Spectator Yearbook. New York: F. A. Stokes, 1934, pp. 172-74.

312. "Tom Grey Could So Easily Lead Them." Today, 1 (24 March 1934), pp. 8-9, 23.

313. "Tough Babes in the Woods." Today, 1 (10 February 1934), pp. 6-7, 22.

314. "The Triumph of a Modern." New Republic, 33 (31 January 1923), pp. 245-47.

315.   "The Triumph of the Egg.." Dial, 68 (March 1920), pp. 295-304.

316.   "Two Lovers." Story, 14 (January-February 1939), pp. 16-25.

317.   "Unlighted Lamps." Smart Set, 65 (July 1921), pp. 45-55.

318.   "The Untold Lie." Seven Arts, 1 (January 1917), pp. 215-21.

319.   "V. F. Calverton." Modern Quarterly, 11, No. 7 (Fall 1940), p. 41.

320.   "Valley Apart." Today, 3 (20 April 1935), pp. 6-7, 22-23.

321.   "Vibrant Life." Little Review, 3 (March 1916), pp. 10-11.

322.   "Village Wassail." Today, 3 (26 January 1935), pp. 8-9, 20.

323.   "Virginia." Vanity Fair, 32 (August 1929), pp. 66, 74.

324.   "Virginia Justice." Today, 2 (21 July 1934), pp. 6-7, 24.

325.   "War of the Winds." Today, 3 (23 February 1935), pp. 8-9, 20.

326.   "We Are All Small-towners." This Week (16 June 1940), p. 2.

327.   "We Would Be Wise: Talking It Out." Agricultural Advertising, 10 (January 1903), pp. 45-47.

328.   "What Makes a Boy Afraid." Woman's Home Companion, 54 (January 1927), pp. 19-20, 96.

329.   "When America Goes to War: A Symposium." Modern Monthly, 9 (June 1935), p. 201.

330.   "When Are Authors Insulted?" Bookman, 75 (October 1932), p. 564.

331. "When I Left Business for Literature." Century, 108
      (August 1924), pp. 489-96.

332. "When the Writer Talks." New York Evening Post
      Literary Review (18 April 1925), pp. 1-2.

333. "When We Care." Twice a Year, 10/11 (Spring-
      Summer/Fall-Winter 1943), pp. 238-44.

334. "The White Streak." Smart Set, 55 (July 1918), pp.
      27-30.

335. "Whither the American Writer: A Questionnaire."
      Modern Quarterly, 6, No. 2 (Summer 1932), p. 12.

336. "Why I Live Where I Live." Golden Book, 16 (No-
      vember 1932), pp. 398-400.

337. "Why I Write." Writer, 49 (December 1936), pp.
      363-64.

338. "Why Men Write." Story, 8 (January 1936), pp. 2,
      4, 103, 105.

339. "Why There Must Be a Midwestern Literature."
      Vanity Fair, 16 (March 1921), pp. 23-24.

340. "Why They Got Married." Vanity Fair, 32 (March
      1929), pp. 74, 116.

341. "Winter Day's Walk in New York." American Specta-
      tor, 2, No. 15 (January 1934), p. 3.

342. "A Word of Advice." Literary Workshop, 1, No. 2
      (1934), p. 43.

343. "Worlds of Fancy and of Facts." Woman's Home
      Companion, 53 (September 1926), pp. 27-28, 79.

344. "A Writer's Conception of Realism." Writer, 54
      (January 1941), pp. 3-6.

345. "A Writer's Notes." New Masses, 8 (August 1932),
      p. 10.

346. "Writing It Down." Agricultural Advertising, 9
      (November 1902), p. 46.

347.   "The Yellow Gown." Mademoiselle, 15 (September
        1942), pp. 94-95, 154-57.

348.   "Young Man From West Virginia." Today, 3 (1 De-
        cember 1934), pp. 5, 23-24.

                D. INTRODUCTIONS, FOREWORDS,
                   AND MISCELLANEOUS WORKS

349.   Alfred Stieglitz Presents 7 Americans: A Catalogue
        of an Exhibition at the Anderson Galleries, New York,
        March 9-28, 1925. New York: Alfred Stieglitz,
        1925. Introduction, p. 3.

350.   Crane, Stephen. The Works of Stephen Crane, XI:
        Midnight Sketches and Other Impressions. New York:
        Alfred A. Knopf, 1926. Introduction, pp. xi-xv.

351.   Dreiser, Theodore. Free and Other Stories. New
        York: Modern Library, 1918. Introduction, pp. v-x.

352.   Jolas, Eugene. Cinema. New York: Adelphi, 1926.
        Introduction, pp. 9-10.

353.   Maurer, Alfred H. An Exhibition of Paintings by
        Alfred H. Maurer, Beginning January Fifteenth 1924.
        New York: Weyhe, 1924. Essay.

354.   McKee, Philip. Big Town. New York: Day, 1931.
        Foreword, pp. 1-9.

355.   Shaw, Lloyd. Cowboy Dances. Caldwell, Idaho:
        Caxton Printers, 1939. Foreword, p. 5.

356.   Sklar, George and Albert Maltz. Peace on Earth.
        New York and Los Angeles: Samuel French, 1934.
        Foreword, pp. v-vi.

357.   Stein, Gertrude. Geography and Plays. Boston:
        Four Seas, 1922. Introduction.

358.   Whitman, Walt. Leaves of Grass. New York:
        Thomas Y. Crowell, 1933. Introduction, pp. v-vii.

E. LETTERS

359. "The Herald Angel Sings." New York Times (10 December 1933), p. 4.

360. "Letter to V. F. Calverton." Modern Quarterly, 2 (Fall 1924), p. 81.

361. "Letters from SA." In Paul Rosenfeld, Voyager in the Arts. Jerome Mellquist and Lucie Wiese, eds. New York: Creative Age, 1948, pp. 197-232.

362. The Letters of Sherwood Anderson. Howard Mumford Jones and Walter B. Rideout, eds. Boston: Little, Brown, 1953.

363. "The Letters of SA." Atlantic Monthly, 191 (June 1953), pp. 30-33.

364. "Letters of SA." Berkeley, 1 (1947), pp. 1-4.

365. "Letters of SA." Harper's Bazaar, 73 (February 1949), pp. 201-03.

366. "Letters to Gertrude Stein." In The Flowers of Friendship: Letters Written to Gertrude Stein. Donald Gallup, ed. New York: Alfred A. Knopf, 1953.

367. "Letters to Van Wyck Brooks." Story, 19 (September-October 1941), pp. 42-62.

368. SA/Gertrude Stein, Correspondence and Personal Essays. Ray Lewis White, ed. Chapel Hill: University of North Carolina Press, 1972.

F. SERIAL PUBLICATIONS EDITED BY SA

369. American Spectator. New York. December 1933-March 1935. Co-Editor.

370. Commercial Democracy. Elyria, Ohio. 1909?-1910. Editor.

371. Marion Democrat. Marion, Virginia. November
      1927-1929. Editor.

372. Smyth County News. Marion, Virginia. November
      1927-1929. Editor.

G. SPECIAL COLLECTIONS

373. The Anderson Collection at the Newberry Library
      of Chicago: By far the most significant collection of
      Anderson's papers, the Newberry Collection numbers
      16,718 items gathered in 144 boxes. Items are ar-
      ranged in four sections: 1) outgoing letters, chrono-
      logically arranged; 2) incoming letters and assorted
      material relative to SA, alphabetically ordered; 3)
      works by SA, arranged alphabetically; and 4) appendix:
      (a) art work, (b) development project, (c) dust jacket
      collection, (d) photographs, (e) reserved boxes, and
      (f) sealed boxes. Among the most significant manu-
      scripts available to scholars are Winesburg, Ohio,
      Beyond Desire, Many Marriages, and Marching Men.
      The collection of letters includes more than 3,000 let-
      ters written by Anderson and more than 7,000 written
      to him. Gathered amidst the scores of unpublished
      manuscripts are fascinating fragments, tentative
      sketches and notes for short stories and the lengthy
      texts of two unfinished novels, Talbot Whittingham
      and Mary Cochran.

374. The Anderson Collection at the Clifton Walter Barrett
      Library: The Collection includes over sixty items of
      Anderson correspondence, photographs, and manu-
      scripts.

PART II

SECONDARY MATERIALS

A. BOOKS OF BIOGRAPHY, SCHOLARSHIP, AND CRITICISM

375. Anderson, David D. SA: An Introduction and Interpretation. New York: Holt, Rinehart, and Winston, 1967.
    In his excellent book-length study David D. Anderson argues that "Anderson's works, in all their variety of forms, from short story to essay to novel to autobiographical memoir, must be approached as a unit; that the works as a whole provide the record of one man's attempt to understand the relation between the individual and the time in which he lived and to determine the ultimate meaning of that relation" (3). Mr. Anderson examines chronologically all of SA's published works and certain unpublished ones, and also brings significant extrinsic biographical information to bear. Anderson asserts that the essence of SA's philosophy lies in his deep-rooted concern for breaking through the walls of human isolation that prevent meaningful communication. Sherwood Anderson no doubt realized that man is destined to live his life isolated within the walls of self. But he also realized the high truth that there are moments when man shatters the walls, sees beneath the surface of reality, and knows the quiet ecstasy of pure and total love and understanding. Anderson suggests the simplest and perhaps most profound truth which recurs throughout the works of SA: "Through compassion and through empathic understanding, man could break down the barriers that separated him from his fellows. In the process he would recognize the true values in human life, the understanding and love that, mutually achieved, would make life worth living" (167).

376. Burbank, Rex. SA. New York: Twayne, 1964.
    Burbank's book offers both biographical and critical assessments of Anderson. The opening chapter examines "those facts of Anderson's life that shaped the essential configurations of his tales and romances and that formed the attitudes that became his themes" (Preface). The seven chapters that follow analyze Anderson's major novels, short story

47

collections, and A Story Teller's Story. Burbank omits Tar,
Death in the Woods, and some other shorter pieces either because they are easily understandable in light of discussion of
the more significant works, or because they lack enduring
literary qualities. While noting a discouragingly long list of
Anderson's failures, Burbank nonetheless concludes with high
praise: "No other writer has portrayed so movingly the
emerging consciousness of the culturally underprivileged Mid-
westerner and has done it, for the most part, with neither
condescension nor satiric caricature" (141). Anderson's relatively small quantity of first-rate work assures him "a
most significant and enduring place in the literature of the
twentieth century" (143).

377.   Chase, Cleveland B.   SA.   New York: R. M. Mc-
        Bride, 1927.
            Cleveland B. Chase bases his conception of Ander-
son upon the thirteen volumes of poetry, fiction, essays, and
autobiography written by Anderson before 1927. He dismiss-
es the two volumes of poetry, Tar, and all but one of his
first five novels as works that "fail to come up to a very
high standard of accomplishment" (74). Dark Laughter is
only a shade better than the four novels already dismissed,
and A Story Teller's Story--while no doubt an interesting
book of reminiscences--will not likely warrant a very high
"literary rating" (75). Only a few of the stories in The
Triumph of the Egg and Horses and Men "escape the blue
pencil" (75), which leaves only Winesburg, Ohio, upon which,
Chase believes, Anderson's reputation must stand or fall.
Even Winesburg is only partially successful. There Anderson "seemed on the verge of penetrating imaginatively beneath the surface" (84) of reality, but ultimately he "was un-
equal to the task. To the pure metal of genuine inspiration
he preferred cheap substitutes and so returned to his world
of thin romanticism and sentimentality" (84).

378.   Fagin, Nathan Bryllion.   The Phenomenon of SA: A
        Study of American Life and Letters.   Baltimore:
        Rossi-Bryn, 1927.
            Fagin offers a highly personal, purely arbitrary
response to the decade of Anderson's writing between 1916
and 1926. He believes that Anderson summarizes a vital
period of American history. As he notes in his Preface,
"I have sought to understand the phenomenon in American
life and letters that is SA. I have sought to relate, just as
he has related what he has found in life, what I have found
in him" (ix). Fagin finds within the middle-aged, midwest-

ern body of SA, "the soul of an adolescent" (16), the young,
alive thing deep inside that prevents his becoming a grotesque.   Like the old man in "The Book of the Grotesque,"
Anderson has a "young, rebellious spirit inside" (17) that
saves him and gives credence to his artistic utterings.
Mostly, Fagin is impressed by the genuineness he finds in
Anderson and by Anderson's ability to "appeal to lonely people in a world of thickly populated isolation" (126).   Finally,
he appreciates the simplicity and power of Anderson's characters where "hearts ... are as full of the pathos and beauty
of life as the hearts of any people that have ever been portrayed in American fiction or narrative verse" (143).

379.   Howe, Irving. SA: A Biographical and Critical
        Study. New York: William Sloan, 1951.
            Still among the most important of the Anderson
critical canon, Howe's book places Anderson as an essentially minor writer who occasionally achieved moments of genius.
According to Howe, "Anderson never wrote a completely sat-
isfying novel" (viii), but in Winesburg, a handful of short
stories, and the first section of Poor White he wrote bril-
liantly, even greatly.   Howe offers biographical, bibliographical, and critical commentary, and his book simply must be
referred to in any serious Andersonian research.   His chapter, "The Book of the Grotesque," remains a particularly
discerning essay on Winesburg, Ohio.

380.   Schevill, James. SA: His Life and Work.   Denver:
        University of Denver Press, 1951.
            Schevill's thoughtfully organized, highly readable
biography affords a warm, yet intellectually discerning portrait of SA.   Schevill offers a tasteful blend of humorous
and interesting anecdotes with calm recital of fact and penetrates the romantic myths surrounding the life of an artist
who pursued the creative life of letters and abandoned the
soul-stultifying world of business.   The Anderson Schevill
paints is a fine advertising copy writer, a flashy dresser, a
lover of men and women everywhere, a storyteller, an artist capable of moments of genius and in the end, a courageous
man who believed, "Life not Death, is the Great Adventure."

381.   Sutton, William A. Exit to Elsinore.   Muncie, Indi-
        ana: Ball State University, 1967.
            A tediously researched biographical monograph
covering the years 1907-1913, the time of Anderson's resi-
dence in Elyria, Ohio.   The title, "Exit to Elsinore," derives from a letter sent by Anderson to his wife Cornelia on

30 November 1912 and apparently written while SA was suffering from amnesia. (On 1 December 1912 Anderson had
been found dazed and suffering from nervous exhaustion in
Cleveland, Ohio.) The realm of Elsinore is seen as psychologically akin to the realm of escape.

381a. Sutton, William A. The Road to Winesburg. Me-
       tuchen, New Jersey: Scarecrow Press, 1972.
       Sutton traces the development of Anderson's ideas
leading to the writing of his masterpiece, Winesburg, Ohio.
The book includes several hundred previously unpublished
letters and informative interviews with Anderson intimates.

382.   Weber, Brom. SA. Minneapolis: University of
       Minnesota Press, 1964.
       Highly readable, concise, biographical and critical
portrait. Provides insightful overview of Anderson's work,
offering perceptive, if necessarily brief, comments on SA's
major artistic strengths and weaknesses. Weber concurs
with William Faulkner that Anderson has not yet received his
"proper evaluation." Useful selective bibliography.

                          B. MEMOIRS

383.   Anderson, Elizabeth and Gerald R. Kelly. Miss
       Elizabeth: A Memoir. Boston: Little, Brown, 1969,
       pp. 34-35, 41, 47-195ff.

384.   Anderson, Margaret. My Thirty Years' War. New
       York: Covici, Friede, 1930, pp. 38-39. 1930; rpt.
       Westport, Connecticut: Greenwood Press, 1971.
       In her chapter, "The Little Review," Ms. Ander-
son recalls her year as literary editor of that Chicago magazine and her conversations with members of an informal literary group that included Anderson, Floyd Dell, Theodore
Dreiser, and others. She remembers Anderson as a "talker
and of a highly special type. He didn't talk ideas--he told
stories" (38). He apparently read to the Dells and Ms. Anderson the entire manuscript of Windy McPherson's Son. She
recalls, "Floyd was passionate about it--I, a little less so.
It was new prose but I knew by Sherwood's look that he would
do something even better" (39).

385.   Beach, Sylvia. Shakespeare and Company. New York:

Harcourt, Brace, 1959, pp. 30-32.
Anderson met Sylvia Beach in Paris shortly after
the publication of Winesburg, Ohio, in 1919. Speaking no
French, he enlisted her aid in business conversations with
his French publishers, the Nouvelle Revue Française.
Through Ms. Beach, Anderson also met Gertrude Stein, an
event that receives marvelous comic treatment as Beach
describes the tribulations of Tennessee Anderson (Sherwood's
second wife) who tried in vain to partake of the conversation
between the two writers. Ms. Stein apparently had standing
orders against the presence of wives of literary visitors.

386.   Boyd, James. "A Man in Town. " Story, 19 (Sep-
        tember-October 1941), pp. 88-91.
        Boyd remembers Anderson's visits to Southern
Pines and the impression he made on people of the town.
He was seen as a small-town man, but as much more than
that. He was a creature of inexhaustible interests, a master of small talk, but most importantly, a man of perfect
freedom and integrity.

387.   Brooks, Van Wyck. An Autobiography. New York:
        Dutton, 1965, pp. 259, 263-67, 269, 272, 358, 363,
        458.
        Brooks touches upon biography and criticism,
writing of Anderson and his fiction as both friend and critic.
It is the friend who takes Anderson's "dreams" with a grain
of salt, and the critic who perceives an occasional artificial
simplicity such as Hemingway took for affectation in The Torrents of Spring.

388.   Carnevali, Emanuel. The Autobiography of Emanuel
        Carnevali. Ed. Kay Boyle. New York: Horizon
        Press, 1967, pp. 14, 168-70, 177, 183, 185, 251.
        In rather loose, stream-of-consciousness, flowing
prose, Carnevali recalls early years in Chicago when he and
Anderson and Waldo Frank occasionally visited "The Dill
Pickle," a little club that was "the fair of freaks, the union
of eccentrics, the forum of those who arrived the wrong moment, were wrongly welcomed, and came to the wrong place"
(168). He enjoyed a pleasant relationship with Sherwood and
Tennessee Anderson that was marred by only one event. One
evening when seemingly every "vestige of reality had left"
(176) him, Carnevali staggered and stumbled to Anderson's
home. Sherwood attempted to relax him by giving him food,
but when the madness persisted he "fairly chased me [Carne-
vali] out of the house" (177).

389.   Dahlberg, Edward. Alms for Oblivion. Minneapolis:
        University of Minnesota Press, 1964, pp. 3-19.
        Dahlberg offers a number of perfectly arbitrary
and interesting observations of Anderson in his opening chapter, "My Friends Streglitz, Anderson, and Dreiser." He recalls Anderson and Ford Madox Ford as "sex visionaries"
(10) who "understood people because they touched them" (10).
This heightened tactile sense is a key to understanding Anderson, "who did not have a great head, but whose flesh was
always growing and ripening for others" (10). Dahlberg
further contends that Anderson "cowered before money, fear-
ing it might destroy what was fecund in him" (10-11), and he
relates one fascinating anecdote about the home Anderson
built near Marion, Virginia. It seems that Sherwood wanted
to go to Virginia "to be humble and get away from money"
(11), but that he had paid the workmen who constructed his
home such high wages that the "people in the town were bitter in their complaints: they said that before he had come
there was none of that northern city dollar discontent in Marion" (11).

390.   Dell, Floyd. Homecoming. New York: Farrar and
        Rinehart, 1933, pp. 236-37.
        In his chapter, "Last Days in Chicago," Floyd
Dell remembers Sherwood Anderson, a "hitherto unknown
novelist" (236) who approached him with the manuscript for
Windy McPherson's Son, which Dell "immensely admired"
(236). He describes it as a novel that "had things in it
about the Middle West which had never got into fiction, and
a soul-searching quasi-Dostoievskian note in it" (236) that
complemented Dell's own "soul-questioning state of mind"
(237).

391.   Dell, Floyd. "How SA Became an Author." New
        York Herald Tribune Books, 18 (12 April 1942), pp.
        1-2.
        Dell's review of the posthumous Memoirs suggest
that the book be taken as fiction, but fiction "that contains a
great deal of truth about its author" (1). Like most of Anderson's other works, the Memoirs offer "self-revelation,
extraordinarily candid, often touching and beautiful" (1).
Furthermore, the book offers something "never seen in his
earlier writings--humor about SA" (1).

392.   Dell, Floyd. "SA, His First Novel." Looking at
        Life. New York: Knopf, 1924, pp. 79-84.
        Dell recalls stopping by the house of a friend and

seeing a typed manuscript of an unfinished novel. After
reading only a few pages, Dell knew he was in the presence
of a great novelist.   In this short chapter, Dell praises
Windy McPherson's Son not only for its emotional power and
rich humor, but most importantly for its "profound sincerity,
the note of serious, baffled, tragic questioning which I hear
above its laughter and tears" (83).

393.   "Derleth, August. Three Literary Men: A Memoir
        of Sinclair Lewis, Sherwood Anderson, Edgar Lee
        Masters. New York: Candlelight Press, 1963, pp.
        31-36.

394.   Dos Passos, John. The Best Times: An Informal
        Memoir. New York: New American Library, 1966,
        pp. 128-29.
          Dos Passos recalls being introduced to Anderson
by F. Scott Fitzgerald in New York in the early twenties,
and later trying to talk Hemingway out of publishing his
parody, The Torrents of Spring--even though he agreed with
Hemingway about the silly sentimentality of Dark Laughter.

395.   Eastman, Max. "The Great and Small Ernest Heming-
        way." Great Companions: Critical Memoirs of Some
        Famous Friends. New York: Farrar, Straus, and
        Cudahy, 1959, pp. 49-50, 72.
          In a chapter focusing upon Ernest Hemingway,
Eastman comments upon The Torrents of Spring, Hemingway's parody of Anderson, labeling the work "one of the
poorest books ever written. It sits like a puddle of escaped
water in the careful architecture of Hemingway's writings"
(50).

396.   Feibleman, James K. "Memories of SA." Shenando-
        ah, 13 (Apring 1962), pp. 32-45.
          Feibleman recalls his friendship with Anderson in
New Orleans.

397.   Frank, Waldo. "SA." In The American Jungle (1925-
        1936). New York: Farrar and Rinehart, 1937, pp.
        93-96.
          Subjective almost to the point of reverence, Frank
finds Anderson's work "a relation of the search for fresh re-
ligious values; a groping toward an Apocalypse in our own
inchoate terms" (93). Anderson, in Frank's portrait, becomes a kind of primitive, almost phallic, American literary
god.

398.   Frank, Waldo. Our America. New York: Boni and
        Liveright, 1920, pp. 136-44.
        Frank reinforces the Anderson myth, vowing that
Anderson turned away from a successful business career because he "found in himself two growing senses: the sense
of boredom and the sense of shit" (137). SA sought new
meaning in the world of artistic creation.

399.   Galantiere, Lewis. "French Reminiscence." Story.
        19 (September-October 1941), pp. 64-67.
        Galantiere remembers SA's first visit to Paris in
1921 and his accurate preconceptions of the French capital
which derived from reading Eugene Sue's The Mysteries of
Paris. He recalls, too, the problems of Marguerite Gay in
translating Winesburg into French, and a comment of Anderson's on Sinclair Lewis: "Kind of worried about himself because his books sell. He thinks I'm an artist because my
books don't sell; and say, that fellow wants to be an artist
worse than a cow wants to have a calf!" (65).

400.   Garnett, Edward. Friday Nights. New York: Knopf,
        1922, pp. 335-46.

401.   Hansen, Harry. Midwest Portraits. New York:
        Harcourt, 1923, pp. 109-79.
        Hansen remembers the Chicago years: Anderson,
his hair long and shaggy and wearing trousers that bagged at
the knees, would read from the manuscripts of Windy Mc-
Pherson's Son and Marching Men. Other Chicago literary
men--Dreiser and Dell and Llewellyn Jones--listened eagerly,
sympathetically. The literary circle talked of many things,
and Anderson was a voice for new literary forms and above
all, truth and honesty in writing. Hansen observed in Anderson a desire for a "better understanding of people, a
deeper inquiry into their inner selves--the sort of writing
that comes only with an older, introspective civilization"
(115). Part III of Hansen's chapter on Anderson provides
interesting information on the publishing background of Windy
McPherson's Son and Marching Men and insights into two unpublished novels: Mary Cochran and Talbot Whittingham.
Hansen further examines Winesburg, Poor White, The Triumph of the Egg, and other writings.

402.   Hecht, Ben. A Child of the Century. New York:
        Simon and Schuster, 1954, pp. 225-232.
        Hecht's fascinating chapter, "My Friend Swatty,"
begins with Hecht's first meeting with Anderson, who had ar-

rived shaggy-bearded and mentally shaky in Chicago after
abandoning business interests in Elyria, Ohio.   The two
young writers collaborated on a play about Benvenuto Cellini,
but abandoned their efforts after finishing one long act.   Apparently, if Hecht knew little about playwriting, "Sherwood
seemed to know less." Hecht also relates two rather bitter
anecdotes about Anderson: one referring to the attempted
suicide of his Chicago mistress and the second suggesting the
peculiar circumstances of a twenty-year feud between the two
literary men.   In "Some Criticism--And A Carom Shot,"
Hecht comments directly on Anderson as a writer.   He observes that Anderson "was one of the finest poets of our
time" (271) and Hecht appreciates the poetry underlying Anderson's best novels and short stories.   However, Hecht also concludes that Sherwood "had little literary discipline and
hardly any technique....   His plots, when they existed, were
childlike and usually seemed like lies" (231).

403.   Hecht, Ben.   "Don Quixote and His Lost Windmill."
       A Thousand and One Afternoons in Chicago.   Chicago:
       Covici-McGee, 1922, pp. 31-34.
       Hecht relates a very interesting luncheon he had
with Anderson.   A Russian-born Jewish emigrant named
Shlorg spent money lavishly on Anderson, Hecht, and the
other patrons, buying drinks and toasting a future success.
The following day, Anderson spotted a newspaper article
which recorded the Russian's suicide and exposed his masked
financial troubles.

404.   Hemingway, Ernest.   A Moveable Feast.   New York:
       Scribner's, 1964, pp. 25-31.
       Hemingway reminisces about his years in Paris,
working as a correspondent for a Canadian newspaper and
occasionally visiting 27 rue de Fleurus, the home of Gertrude
Stein.   Although Ms. Stein was rather reluctant to discuss
literature, she and Hemingway sometimes talked of Anderson.
Hemingway thought some of his short stories were "beautiful-
ly written" (27-28), but found his novels "strangely poor"
(28) and parodied Dark Laughter in The Torrents of Spring.
Ms. Stein only "began to praise Sherwood lavishly after he
had cracked-up as a writer" (28).

405.   Hind, Charles Lewis.   Authors and I.   New York:
       John Lane, 1921, pp. 19-23.
       Hind arbitrarily comments on each of Anderson's
first four books.   He believes Windy McPherson's Son could
have been written only by an American, for it takes its guts

from the American mid-west experience. <u>Marching Men</u> is
"a remarkable study of a personality emerging from crude
conditions and raw men, envisaging how to head and lead"
(20). Hind suggests <u>Mid-American Chants</u> may be "his most
significant, his most <u>self-expressive book</u>" (21). <u>Winesburg</u>
is a fitting successor of <u>Spoon River Anthology</u>, for while
Masters' book focuses on the past, Anderson's work deals
"with the present and the future" (22).

406. Huddleston, Sisley. <u>Paris Salons, Cafes, Studios</u> ...
      <u>Being Social, Artistic, and Literary Memories.</u> New
      York: Blue Ribbon Books, 1928, pp. 78-82.
      An American expatriate in Paris, Huddleston
describes the visiting Anderson as "The most English of
American writers just as Sinclair Lewis is the most American" (78). He bases his contentions upon the "musical, col-
orful, rich suave, ... flexible and unfolding" (79) style that
is Anderson's and that is English, or perhaps European, in
texture and tradition.

407. Loeb, Harold. <u>The Way It Was.</u> New York: Cri-
      tcrion, 1959, pp. 9, 59, 63, 81, 235, 246.
      Loeb's memoir presents an intimate view of the
literary-intellectual scene of the twenties and thirties, of
which Anderson was an important part.

408. Morris, Lloyd R. <u>Postscript to Yesterday.</u> New
      York: Random House, 1947, pp. 145-48.
      Morris perceives Anderson as a kind of literary
Babbitt "at odds with his environment" (145) and through his
fiction striking out "against an America of speed, hurried
workmanship, cheap automobiles for cheap men, cheap chairs
in cheap houses, city apartments with shiny bathroom floors,
the Ford, the Twentieth Century Limited, the World War,
jazz, the movies" (147). The culmination of Anderson's
piercing vision, <u>Winesburg, Ohio</u>, strips away the veils of
decency from small-town life, revealing "thwarted, lonely,
warped people; shame ridden, and driven at last to a catas-
trophe of sexual abnormality" (145).

409. Rascoe, Burton. <u>Before I Forget.</u> Garden City, New
      Jersey: Doubleday, Doran, 1937, p. 368.
      Rascoe describes a party in Chicago attended by
Sinclair Lewis, Anderson, and other friends of Rascoe's.
Anderson entertained with his Mama Geighen story, a tale
about a fantastic binge of Anderson and George Wharter's and
their encounter with the massive, marvelous Mama who ran

a roadside tavern somewhere in Wisconsin. Anderson, however, had to take second seat to Lewis who parted his hair
severely and powdered his hair white prior to delivering an
"extempore sermon on the evils of drink and on the evil that
women like Mama Geighen do in this world" (368).

410.   Rosenfeld, Paul. "The Man of Good Will. " Story,
        19 (September-October 1941), pp. 5-10.
        In a highly personal reminiscence, Rosenfeld re-
calls Anderson, the man and artist, from their first meeting
in 1917 through the triumph of a long literary career. Rosenfeld perceives SA most affectionately as a man who aimed
for "peace, good will to men" (10).

411.   Stein, Gertrude.   The Autobiography of Alice B. Tok-
        las. New York: Harcourt, Brace, 1933, pp. 241-42.
        The Autobiography recalls Ms. Stein's first meet-
ing with Anderson in her Paris home (see also no. 385,
Sylvia Beach). Embittered by stacks of unpublished manuscripts and "no hope of publication or serious recognition"
(241), Ms. Stein was much cheered by Anderson's visit and
his unreserved praise of her work. Even Anderson probably
never realized "how much his visit meant to her" (242).

412.   Stein, Gertrude. "Sherwood's Sweetness. " Story, 19
        (September-October 1941), p. 63.
        In an almost syrupy remembrance, Stein notes,
"as long as grape sugar is grape sugar and it always is ...
so long will Sherwood be Sherwood" (63).

413.   Young, Stark. "Marginal Note. " Paul Rosenfeld:
        Voyager in the Arts. Mellquist, Jerome and Wiese,
        Lucie, eds. New York: Creative Age Press, 1948,
        pp. 195-97.

C.   SPECIAL JOURNAL ISSUES

414.   American Notes and Queries (September 1976).
        A special issue will honor the centennial of SA's
birth and will be devoted to critical, biographical, and bibliographical notes on Anderson.

415.   The Newberry Library Bulletin, Second series, No.

2 (December, 1948). This issue focuses attention upon Anderson the man as well as writer and includes personal essays by four men--George H. Daugherty, Waldo Frank, Roger Sergel, and Norman Holmes Pearson--who knew SA at different periods in his life. Also included are Raymond D. Gazzi's compilation of bibliographic information and a description of the Newberry's Anderson collection written by editor Lloyd Lewis. Articles are individually listed and annotated in the bibliography.

416. The Newberry Library Bulletin, 6, No. 8 (July 1971). The year 1969 marked the fiftieth anniversary of the publication of Winesburg, Ohio and also was the year in which the Newberry Library Associates completed the purchase of the manuscript of that book and formally presented it to the Library. This special issue commemorates these two events and includes essays by John H. Ferris, Walter B. Rideout, Welford D. Taylor, Richard C. Johnson, and a checklist of Anderson studies, 1959-1969, compiled by Ray Lewis White.

417. Shenandoah, 13 (Spring 1962). This special issue of Shenandoah seeks to elucidate the work of SA and to assist in defining his reputation. Articles by Frederick J. Hoffman, Walter B. Rideout, James K. Feibleman, Jim S. Lowry, and Curtis D. Williams are individually listed and annotated in this bibliography.

418. Story, 19 (September-October 1941). This special issue of Story, devoted to "the greatest contemporary short story writer," includes tributes, reminiscences, critical essays, biographical commentaries, certain of Anderson's published writings, and SA's letters to Van Wyck Brooks. Articles from Story are listed individually in this bibliography.

D. ARTICLES OF SCHOLARSHIP AND CRITICISM

1. General

419. Almy, Robert F. "SA: The Nonconforming Re-Discoverer." The Saturday Review of Literature, 28 (6

January 1945), pp. 17-18.

420. Anderson, David D. "SA After 20 Years. " <u>Midwest</u>
<u>Quarterly</u>, 3 (January 1962), pp. 119-32.
David D. Anderson assesses the whole of Anderson's work, examining recurring themes and motifs and dis-
cussing misunderstandings that have resulted from critical
harshness on the one hand, and sentimentality stemming from
identification with the problems underlying the myth of the
writer's life on the other. Anderson sought to penetrate appearance and to understand the nature of human experience
beneath it. His success persists in the best of his work,
which David Anderson asserts includes not only <u>Winesburg</u>
but the whole of the short story collections <u>The Triumph of</u>
<u>the Egg</u> and <u>Horses and Men</u>, and later works such as <u>Kit</u>
<u>Brandon</u>, <u>Death in the Woods</u>, the <u>Memoirs</u>, <u>Hello Towns!</u>,
and <u>Puzzled America.</u>

421. Anderson, David D. "SA and the Two Faces of
America. " <u>Critical Studies in American Literature:</u>
<u>A Collection of Essays.</u> Karachi, Pakistan: Univer-
sity of Karachi, 1964, pp. 97-107.
David D. Anderson observes that SA dealt with
three major themes in the first fifteen years of his literary
career: 1) rebellion against American materialism, 2) human isolation, and 3) the nature of reality beneath super-
ficial appearances. Critics have tended to neglect later
writings, but David Anderson suggests SA's later works contained some of his "most perceptive observations and force-
ful writing" (102). During the depression years, SA contributed greatly both to the cause of struggling labor and to
the "cause of a bewildered country" (103). <u>Beyond Desire,</u>
<u>No Swank,</u> and <u>Puzzled America</u> comprise SA's most serious
attempts to come to grips with what David Anderson terms
the "two faces of America--the real, a land of material well-
being, and the ideal, a land in which the individual could find
his fullest human expression" (102).

422. Anderson, David D. "SA's Idea of the Grotesque. "
<u>Ohioana</u>, 6 (Spring 1963), pp. 12-13.
David D. Anderson traces Anderson's use of the
word "grotesque" to an experimental play, titled "Grotesque,"
written by Cloyd Head and Maurice Brown. Anderson was
no doubt familiar with the play, which was first produced at
the Chicago Little Theatre in 1915 and reviewed in the same
issue of <u>The Little Review</u> that carried Anderson's short
story, "Sister. " Anderson notes, "In the play a sardonic

artist manipulates the characters, who are presented as
marionettes, freely, without their understanding what is happening to them" (13). Essentially, this is the position of
Anderson's grotesques in Winesburg. When the characters
in the play discover what is happening to them, they rebel
and gain their freedom. The play's characters foreshadow
the direction taken by later Andersonian grotesques "who
rebel against convention before going on to attempted liberation and fulfillment" (13).

423.   Anderson, David D. "SA's Use of the Lincoln Theme."
       Lincoln Herald, 64 (Spring 1961), pp. 28-32.
             David D. Anderson suggests that throughout SA's
writing career, "he identified the American experience that
he was trying to define with the Lincoln legend that he felt
epitomized it" (28). SA apparently felt a kind of spiritual
kinship with Lincoln. He wrote to Van Wyck Brooks, "I
have myself understood the trenchant sadness of Lincoln"
(28). Anderson argues at some length about the influence of
the Lincoln legend on SA's creation of Hugh McVey in Poor
White and Windy and Sam McPherson in Windy McPherson's
Son. He suggests a continued influence in Tar, A Story
Teller's Story, and Dark Laughter. Anderson's most overt
handling of the Lincoln theme appears in an unfinished study,
"Father Abraham: A Lincoln Fragment."

424.   Anderson, Karl. "My Brother, SA." Saturday Re-
       view of Literature, XXXI (4 September 1948), pp. 6-
       7, 26-27.
             Karl Anderson, a painter and Sherwood's elder
brother, writes a fascinating remembrance of SA, touching
upon their family background, their boyhood in Clyde, SA's
first meeting with Floyd Dell, the publication of Windy Mc-
Pherson's Son, the creation of Winesburg, and their tragic
brother Earl.

425.   Barker, Russell H. "The Storyteller Role." College
       English, 3 (February 1942), pp. 433-44.
             Believing that Anderson's "achievements as a
novelist fall far below his achievements in the field of the
short story" (434), Barker concentrates upon analysis of SA
as a short storyteller, focusing particularly upon the strengths
and weaknesses of his narrative techniques. Barker finds
major structural flaws in "Hands," "The Triumph of the
Egg," and "Death in the Woods," but asserts that "I'm a
Fool" and "I Want to Know Why" are free from glaring narrative flaws. In these two stories, "The hypothetical teller

of the story is also the central character and is, therefore, telling a story about himself (440). This framework afforded Anderson "few opportunities to go astray" (440). Barker concludes that "artistry of a high order Anderson never did achieve" (442), and that through structural analysis, the perceptive critic can observe the "really serious flaws" (442) that mar Anderson's artistic endeavors.

426. Bishop, John Peale. "This Distrust of Ideas (D. H. Lawrence and SA)." Vanity Fair (December 1921), pp. 10-12, 118.

Bishop argues that Anderson, like Lawrence, is "interested in searching out what men hide from the world, in probing under worm-riddled floors and ransacking blind attics" (11). The Triumph of the Egg shows Anderson intensely concerned with the private struggles of the soul--also a topic of interest to Lawrence. But in Lawrence the struggle is rooted in a male-female dichotomy while in "Anderson, it is between some dream of impossible loveliness, which the dreamer wishes to attach to the body of the beloved, and the inane fecundity of life" (11).

427. Blankenship, Russell. American Literature as an Expression of the National Mind. New York: Holt, 1935, pp. 665-72.

Blankenship associates Anderson and Sinclair Lewis "with the revolt against the village" (665). Blankenship's overview of Anderson is highly critical: Anderson's "two difficulties, that of discovering the elusive thing that he is looking for and that of finding words with which to describe it, keep him from becoming a facile writer. He is never brilliant, and indeed succeeds only occasionally" (665). Blankenship includes among the occasional successes some of the Winesburg tales and a few of the stories in The Triumph of the Egg.

428. Bridgeman, Richard. The Colloquial Style in America. New York: Oxford University Press, 1966, pp. 152-64.

Bridgeman notes the influence of Mark Twain--particularly Huckleberry Finn--on Anderson and discusses Anderson's penchant for a stylistically simple American prose fiction, a conscious "bias for artlessness" (153), and a championing of the story teller's seeming spontaneity.

429. Brinnin, John Malcolm. The Third Rose: Gertrude Stein and Her World. Boston: Little, Brown, 1959, pp. 235-38.

In his biography of Gertrude Stein, Brinnin comments on the nature of her relationship with Anderson.
From their first meeting in her Paris apartment, the two
writers formed a mutual admiration society. Though they
seldom met during the course of their lives afterwards, they
maintained an intimate correspondence, encouraging and
praising one another in their literary endeavors. Brinnin
finds a certain affinity in the works of the two Americans,
"a shared striving to bring into literature something beyond
the means of literature--in Anderson's case, the attempt to
make words do the messianic offices of something as vague
as the religion of humanity, and in Gertrude Stein's case,
the determination to make words do what only painting or
the cinema can do" (237).

430. Brossard, Chandler. "SA: A Sweet Singer, 'A
      Smooth Son of a Bitch.'" American Mercury, 72
      (May 1951), pp. 611-16.
      Brossard offers some rather interesting observa-
tions on the oral storyteller technique of Winesburg before
positing psychoanalytic perceptions of Anderson, who, according to Brossard, harbored an Oedipus complex (thus,
four wives--all mother types), an almost neurotic dependence
on friendships, and a "morbid fear of intellect and intellectu-
als" (611). The title of the article derives from Anderson's
concept of the con man he found in himself: "the truth is I
was a smooth son of a bitch." Brossard closes with mixed
reaction to Irving Howe's book (no. 379) on Anderson.
Brossard strongly disagrees with Howe's stated reason for
Anderson becoming a writer. He calls Howe's notion "the
silliest damn statement I've heard in years" (616).

431. Burnett, Whit and Hallie Burnett, eds. Story Jubilee.
      Garden City: Doubleday, 1965, pp. x, 13.
      The Burnetts reprint Anderson's "Two Lovers,"
which first appeared in Story in January, 1939. A brief
homage to Anderson's influence of American short story
writing follows the text of his story.

432. Burrow, Trigant. "Psychoanalytic Improvisations and
      the Personal Equation." Psychoanalytic Review, XIII
      (April 1926), pp. 173-86.
      Burrow recalls a discussion with Anderson in
which he championed the use of psychoanalytic techniques in
probing the human personality while Anderson argued vigor-
ously that human life was not to be got at with surgical, sci-
entific probes. Burrow was so certain he was right that he

undertook an analysis of Anderson; SA argued his point of view in "Seeds. " Their two different positions define the "circumspect psychiatrist and the inquisitive psychoanalyst proper" (174). Each position "owed itself, though unacknowledged, to the personal, equation that secretly actuated" (174) them. What is needed, argues Burrows, is for the two positions to merge "in the mutual observation of their own processes as they involve their own personal equations and to bring their several improvisations to a common analysis through the consensual method of observation through an organized laboratory technique" (186). The psychiatrist will thus arrive at better psychology; the artist, at better artistry.

433. Calverton, Victor F. The Liberation of American Literature. New York: Scribner's, 1932, pp. 425-30 and passim. (reprint, New York: Octagon Books, 1973).

Calverton argues that Anderson has worked and reworked one major theme: "the change which has come over the West with the coming of industrialism" (426). What distinguishes Anderson from other writers who have written on the same theme is his tendency to deal with the "more wistful side of that tragedy instead of the more gruesome" (426), and his depiction of characters that are essentially introspective, representing in their inward struggles "the last attempt of the individual to save his individualism in a world that harassed it whatever direction he turned" (426).

434. Calverton, Victor F. "SA: A Study in Sociological Criticism. " Modern Quarterly, 2 (Fall 1924), pp. 82-118.

Sociological in method, Calverton attempts to analyze "those forces in the social environment that have created the very aesthetic tendencies and concepts which are embodied" (85) in the works of Anderson. Calverton theorizes that the industrial revolution of the 19th century and the consequent organization of the proletariat made possible the interest of Anderson and other artists in the nature and inherent human qualities of the working man. Changing social conditions, Calverton argues, enabled artists to "give the proletarian the tender and meditative consideration, from an aesthetic point of view, that he now receives" (91). Anderson, in Calverton's view, becomes "the orator of the proletarian movement" (91). Through nearly all of Anderson's major fiction throbs "the spirit of the new generation beating racily and importantly" (118).

435.   Cargill, Oscar. "The Primitivists. " Intellectual
        America. New York: Macmillan, 1941, pp. 311-98.
        (reprint, New York: Cooper Square, 1968).
        Although Windy McPherson's Son and Marching
Men add little to what Cargill terms American primitivism,
Winesburg is an altogether different thing. Cargill disagrees
with those critics who find Anderson's chief influence in
Masters' Spoon River Anthology. Winesburg is indeed a revolt-from-the-village work, but more importantly it is a book
marked by a "conscious simplicity of style" influenced by
Gertrude Stein's Three Lives. Poor White, Anderson's next
book, is "a step backward" (327), but The Triumph of the
Egg and Horses and Men are more successful because Anderson has developed "a working knowledge of psychoanalysis
and a modified primitivism" (327).

436.   Collins, Carvel, ed. "Introduction. " William Faulk-
        ner: New Orleans Sketches. New York: Random
        House, 1968, pp. xi-xxxiv.
        Collins' essay offers a concise history of the
Faulkner-Anderson relationship, focusing particular attention
on initial contact in the French Quarter of New Orleans.

437.   Crane, Hart. "SA. " Double Dealer, 2 (July 1921),
        pp. 42-44.
        Crane finds in Anderson's works a stark realism
that penetrates to the essence of animal and earthly life, and
he recognizes Anderson as "among the few first recorders
of the life of a people coming to some state of self-con-
sciousness" (44).

438.   Crawford, Nelson Antrim. "SA, the Wistfully Faith-
        ful. " Midland, 8 (November 1922), pp. 297-308.
        Crawford examines Anderson's short story, "Sis-
ter," and suggests that even in this early work Anderson
displayed three qualities that place his work among the
finest produced in the twenties: 1) a flowing, natural style,
2) a "feeling for the tragedy of current American life--a
tragedy chiefly of frustration" (298), and 3) a distinct mystical symbolism. Crawford reserves high praise for Winesburg and is surprisingly impressed with A New Testament:
there he finds "Anderson himself, revealing himself as no
American except Whitman has ever revealed himself" (306).

439.   Daugherty, George. "Anderson, Advertising Man. "
        Newberry Library Bulletin, Series II, No. 2 (Decem-
        ber 1948), pp. 30-43.

Daugherty, editor of the Republic-Times in Springfield, Ohio, roomed at "The Oaks" where Anderson worked as chore boy in 1899. He recalls that Harry Simmons, advertising manager of the Crowell firm, sent Sherwood to the company's Chicago office to sell advertising under the direction of Joe Ford. Anderson became dissatisfied with the staid, monotonous office routine, and with the help of Marco Morrow, formerly of Springfield, secured a job with the Frank B. White Advertising Agency where he remained until 1906. Anderson wrote a number of articles in Agricultural Advertising in two columns, "Business Types" and "Rot and Reason."

440. Dickie, Francis. "From Forest Fire to France." American Book Collector, 10 (October 1959), pp. 23-24. (Subtitled: "SA and the Photographic Eye.")

Dickie recalls meeting Anderson in Paris and a late dinner conversation during which Anderson shared his views on writing for dollars: "It is the great illusion that you can write cheap stuff, popular stuff, in order to earn the money to give you time to write greatly. Hundreds of writers in America proceed on that assumption. But it is a false one" (24).

441. Dickinson, L. R. "Smyth County Items." Outlook, 148 (11 April 1928), pp. 581-83.

Dickinson airs Marion views of Sherwood Anderson, editor of both the Marion Democrat and the Smyth-County News. One interesting anecdote recalls Anderson's fervid support of the local town band. After a few weeks of editorializing, "contributions poured in from Mr. Otto Kahn, from Horace Liveright, ... from Henry Mencken, and others. The town was amazed" (581). Residents of Marion were initially uneasy about the national attention consequent to Anderson's editorship, but in the end were pleased to be placed on the map. Says Dickinson, "we don't care one chinquapin from the slopes of Molly's knob" (582) about having Marion rusticity spread abroad.

442. Dreiser, Theodore. "SA." Story, 19 (September-October 1941), pp. 4.

In fond remembrance Dreiser says of Anderson, "Whenever I think of him I think of that wondrous line out of 'The Ancient Mariner'--'He prayeth best who loveth best all things both great and small'" (4).

443. Drew, Elizabeth A. The Modern Novel. London:

Jonathan Cape, 1926, pp. 147-48 and passim.
Ms. Drew perceives Anderson as a kind of American D. H. Lawrence, "struggling to say something for which
at present he has not found the mode of expression" (147).

444.   Duffey, Bernard. "The Struggle for Affirmation--
       Anderson, Sandburg, Lindsay." The Chicago Renais-
       sance in American Letters. Lansing: Michigan State
       College Press, 1954, pp. 194-309. (reprint, The
       Achievement of SA. Ray Lewis White, ed. Chapel
       Hill: University of North Carolina Press, 1966, pp.
       46-59.)
       Duffey points to the Elyria amnesia episode, An-
derson's flight from business, and his many marriages as
establishing a biographical pattern that is intrinsically related to the style and structure of his fiction. More importantly, however, it suggests a sensitive, probing search
for "a sense of self, to be achieved in the craft of writing"
(197). Anderson's search was greatly aided by his experience as an "explorer of the Liberation" (201) in the Chicago
Renaissance. There he honed a personal theory of art as
successful intuition, "What we have got to do ... is to feel
into things. To do that we only need learn from people that
what they say and think isn't of very much importance" (201).

445.   Edgar, Pelham. The Art of the Novel. New York:
       Macmillan, 1933, pp. 338-51.
       In a chapter devoted to Anderson, Hemingway,
Dos Passos, and Faulkner, Edgar briefly comments on each
writer, noting in part Hemingway's and Faulkner's debt to
Anderson. He finds in Anderson's device of under-statement
"an effective medium of expression giving him control of
quite novel dramatic and poetic effects" (343).

446.   Fadiman, Clifton. "SA: The Search for Salvation."
       Nation, 135 (9 November 1932), pp. 454-56.
       Fadiman points to the phenomenon of the middle-
aged male rediscovering his ego, transporting him back to
the hot fevers and fervors of adolescence, as a key to understanding Anderson and "the whole American experience he
represents" (454). It goes far in explaining the seeming
"confusion" or bewilderment that besets Anderson's characters as they search for some sort of truth, for meaning, for
salvation in the modern world. Anderson's protagonists often
go "looking for truth as if it were something tangible" (454),
but their quests are futile, for the truth they seek is eternal-
ly elusive. In attempting to evaluate Anderson's overall lit-

erary effort, Fadiman perceives several recurring patterns:
an almost sentimental attack against industrialism, an ideal-
ization of pre-industrial America, an escape desire which
might be labeled the Huck Finn dream. Anderson's best
work lies in a handful of stories of the race track and in
Winesburg, his best book. Perhaps more important, though,
is the courageous self-examination Anderson pursued, a kind
of Rousseauesque daring that lent courage to the coming
generation of writers.

447.   Farrell, James T. "A Memoir on SA." Perspective,
       7 (Summer 1954), pp. 83-88.
       Farrell speaks directly: "Sherwood Anderson in-
fluenced and inspired me, perhaps more profoundly than any
other American writer" (83). Without denying Dreiser's influence, he asserts, "it was Anderson who touched me most
deeply" (83). The book which influenced Farrell most was
Tar, because he found in that book "a means of re-affirma-
tion of self" (84-85). In Tar lay "one of the seeds that led
to Studs Lonigan" (85).

448.   Faulkner, William. "Prophets of the New Age: SA."
       Princeton University Library Chronicle, 18 (1957),
       pp. 89-94. (Note: essay was originally printed in
       the 26 April 1925 issue of the Dallas Morning News.)
       Faulkner comments arbitrarily on Anderson's
major fiction. About the characters of Winesburg, Faulkner
writes: "These people live and breathe: they are beautiful
... And behind all of them a ground of fecund earth and
corn in the green spring and the slow, full hot summer and
rigorous masculine winter that hurts it not, but makes it
stronger" (90). Marching Men and Windy McPherson's Son
are disappointing compared to Winesburg, but in Poor White
"the corn still grows" (90), and in Horses and Men, Faulk-
believes Anderson has again found his proper medium: "In
this book there are people, people that walk and live, and
the ancient stout earth that takes his heartbreaking labor and
gives grudgingly, mayhap, but gives an hundredfold" (92).

449.   Faulkner, William. "SA: An Appreciation." At-
       lantic, 191 (June 1953), pp. 27-29. (Reprinted in
       The Achievement of SA. Ray Lewis White, ed.
       Chapel Hill: University of North Carolina Press,
       1966, pp. 194-99.)
       In an appreciative essay that discloses as much
about Faulkner as it does about Anderson, William Faulkner
recalls Anderson the story-teller, the creator of dreams, the

co-author of a mythical descendant of Andrew Jackson--ha'f-horse, half-alligator and later, half-sheep, half-shark--and most importantly, the teacher of artists who advised that to be a writer, one has first got to be what he is, what he was born. Faulkner perceives Anderson as always, openly and honestly, pursuing the exactitude of purity. Because of that uncompromising pursuit, Faulkner sees the older writer as "a giant in an earth populated to a great--too great--extent by pygmies, even if he did make but the two or perhaps three gestures* commensurate with gianthood" (29). (*Winesburg, The Triumph of the Egg, and Horses and Men.)

450.   Feldman, Eugene. "SA's Search." Psychoanalysis, 3, No. 3 (Spring 1955), pp. 44-51.

Feldman summons up an image from Anderson's boyhood as related in Tar where a child throws himself upon the ground and stuffs his mouth with grass in the hope of being transformed into a sheep. "Sherwood Anderson throughout his literary life was to repeat the theme of this act of childhood" (44). He was to search continually for ways to dissolve the barriers that isolate men from one another, seeking the "magic grass" that will "wipe away the feeling of isolation" (45). Anderson, according to Feldman, found two ways to escape isolation: One was "by entering the temple of work"; the other, "by entering the temple of sex" (50). Psychologically the work temple was dedicated to his heavily belabored mother; the sex temple "signified a flight from the mass and a return to the illusion-filled father" (51).

451.   Fenton, Charles A. The Apprenticeship of Ernest Hemingway. New York: Farrar, Straus and Young, 1954, pp. 116-20, 145-50.

Fenton details Hemingway's indebtedness--personal and vocational--to Anderson, who provided the young Hemingway with letters of introduction to friends in Paris, including Gertrude Stein. Hemingway was also influenced by Anderson's short stories, particularly Winesburg. Two early Hemingway stories, "Up in Michigan" and "My Old Man," clearly reflect Hemingway's reading of the older writer.

452.   Flanagan, John T. "Hemingway's Debt to SA." Journal of English and German Philology, 54 (October 1955), pp. 507-20.

Flanagan analyzes Hemingway's The Torrents of Spring which burlesques "the specious profundity of Anderson's characters and the repetition of senseless questions" (514), Anderson's style, and the older writer's technique of "interpolating his own views or comments, disrupting the very point of view he sought to establish" (515). In probing to find an answer to why Hemingway attacked Anderson, Flanagan discards the argument that Hemingway was jealous or resentful. Rather, he suggests that Hemingway may have been amazed by the "supineness of Anderson's character" and no longer impressed by the "vagueness and fluidity" (516) of the background in Anderson's stories. Perhaps, also, Hemingway wished to satirize Anderson's seeming inability to look at himself humorously. Flanagan concludes his essay with an examination of Hemingway's literary debt to Anderson. Although Hemingway finally parodied Anderson, he also owed to him certain of his own stylistic tendencies and his handling of plot.

453.   Flanagan, John T.   "The Permanence of SA." Southwest Review, 35 (Summer 1950), pp. 170-77.
        Flanagan notes the wealth of material on Anderson in the Newberry Library collection and suggests that scholarly research may lead to new evaluations of the author and his work. That possibility aside; Flanagan argues persuasively for an enduring place for Anderson in the history of short fiction, where his essential honesty and integrity served to override any shortcomings he may have had in disciplining the structure of his works.

454.   Frank, Waldo.   "SA: A Personal Note." Newberry Library Bulletin, Series 2, No. 2 (December 1948) pp. 39-43.
        Frank recalls moments in his friendship with Anderson, beginning in late 1915 when Frank, searching for talent for The Seven Arts, wrote to Anderson and received a batch of cheap yellow copy paper bearing the largely unpunctuated draft of "The Untold Lie." Before purchasing the story, Frank asked Anderson if he would consider throwing in a few commas. Anderson only too readily complied, placing "a comma after each half dozen words or so, irrespective of sense" (40). Having witnessed the rise and fall of Anderson's literary star, Frank predicts that the "hour of Sherwood Anderson's definitive integration into American culture should come soon" (43).

455.   Friend, Julius W.   "The Philosophy of SA." Story, 19 (September-October 1941), pp. 37-41.
        Friend argues that Anderson's approach to metaphysics was not that of abstract reasoning, but rather derived from his feeling for the world of experience. Friend

defines SA's philosophy as a kind of "earth mysticism, which
accepts life, the life of the teeming earth, the life of the
senses, as well as the life of the spirit, with something approaching the same kind of ecstasy as that of the Christian
mystics" (37).

456.   Geismar, Maxwell David. "SA: Last of the Towns-
        men." The Last of the Provincials. Boston: Hough-
        ton Mifflin, 1947, pp. 223-84.
        Geismar offers a sympathetic interpretation of
Anderson and his work, finding in Anderson a provincial
American talent sensitive to societal change and continually
searching for that which makes life meaningful. SA's earliest
writing records the agrarian life of small town America in
the throws of the industrial revolution. Anderson's work in
the mid to late 1920's was more introspective, revealing
curious twists of the author's psyche but continuing to assert
a keen cultural insight. Geismar's essay argues strongly for
Anderson's enduring place in the mainstream of modern
American fiction.

457.   Gildzen, Alex. "SA, Elyria, and the Escape Hunch."
        The Serif, 5 (March 1968), pp. 3-10.
        Gildzen examines the influence of the Elyria years
on Anderson's later fiction and argues that the trauma of his
mental "breakdown remained with Anderson, influencing the
creation of John Webster (Many Marriages) and Bruce Dudley
(Dark Laughter) and subtly adding to such characters as
George Willard (Winesburg) and Hugh McVey (Poor White)"
(10).

458.   Gregory, Horace. "Introduction." The Portable
        Sherwood Anderson. 1949; reprint, New York: Viking
        Press, 1967, pp. 1-37.
        Gregory offers a concise overview of Anderson's
life and major works along with a useful chronology and
brief selective bibliography.

459.   Hansen, Harry. "Anderson in Chicago." Story, 19
        (September-October 1941), pp. 34-36.
        Hansen discusses Anderson and the Chicago circle
of artists who were his friends, audience, and constructive
critics. Perhaps SA's greatest achievement during that Chicago period was that he had helped to win an enduring "vic-
tory for honest expression" (36).

460.   Hatcher, Harlan Henthorne. "SA." Creating the

American Novel. New York: Farrar and Rinehart,
1935, pp. 155-71.
 Hatcher places Anderson with Sinclair Lewis and
Theodore Dreiser as the "three most stimulating and influ-
ential authors in the creation of the modern American novel"
(155). Hatcher observes that regardless of genre, Anderson's work is, "in truth, all of a piece.... It is always the
baffled and dreamy boy caught in the tails of poverty and
crudity in any small town; the bewildered men thrust from
old freedoms on the land into factories and industrial life too
complex for their understandings; and the sex-starved vil-
lagers defeated in their private lives because of their eva-
sions, their repressions, and their erotic perversions, and
because they lack the courage to live out their potentialities
in spite of the hostility of their neighbors" (159).

461. Herbst, Josephine. "Ubiquitous Critics and the Au-
       thor." Newberry Library Bulletin, 5 (December
       1958), pp. 1-13.
       Ms. Herbst finds the case of SA particularly ap-
propriate to her discussion regarding the "relation of an author to his critics" (4). Powerful critics may benefit or
abuse, but the massive collection of Anderson papers at the
Newberry Library suggest Anderson "was never able to benefit by the advice of his critics" (4). Ms. Herbst offers interesting insights into the "Chicago Renaissance" era and
underlines the importance of examining the many writers who
are called as well as the few who are chosen if we are "to
understand the climate which nourished possibly an Only One?
How are we to interpret his signs and symbols without ap-
prehending something of that vast family tree upon which his
Golden Apple Hung?" (13).

462. Hicks, Granville. "Two Roads." Great Tradition.
       Rev. ed. New York: Macmillan, 1935, pp. 207-56.
       In his chapter, "Two Roads," Hicks examines
the American literary products of 1912-1925 as a kind of
renaissance of American culture, and he places Anderson
with Dreiser and Lewis as the most important writers of
fiction during that period. More significant than Wharton,
Cather, Cabell, and others, these writers managed to end
"the tyranny of boarding school standards; they substituted
the fresh, natural speech of the people for the language of
books" (237). Anderson's particular strength lay in his
ability to reveal character in a lightning flash, and if "one
were to judge Anderson by only his best work, one could
scarcely avoid the conclusion that his talent was of the first
order" (229).

463.   Hoffman, Frederick J. "The Voices of SA." <u>Shenan-</u>
       <u>doah</u>, 13 (Spring 1962), pp. 5-19.
            According to Hoffman, Anderson produced a small
       body of important work which gives credence to the several
       "voices" through which he addresses the modern world.
       Hoffman perceives four major roles of "voices": 1) advisor
       to contemporary writers; 2) theorist of the imagination and
       creative process; 3) artist of loneliness; and 4) literary his-
       torian of the period of transition and change which occurred
       from about 1870 to 1915.

464.   Howe, Irving. "SA: An American as Artist." <u>Ken-</u>
       <u>yon Review</u>, 13 (Spring 1951), pp. 193-203.
            Howe examines the Anderson legend in the con-
       text of a success-oriented American culture and acknowledges
       in Anderson's prophetic and visionary endeavors a "not un-
       heroic struggle to teach 'anti-success'" (197). He suggests,
       however, a more fruitful way of interpreting Anderson's
       work: "as the expression of a sensitive witness to the na-
       tional experience and as the achievement of a story teller
       who created a small body of fiction unique in American
       writing for the lyrical purity of its feeling" (198).

465.   Ingram, Forrest L. "American Short Story Cycles,
       Foreign Influences and Parallels." <u>Proceedings of</u>
       <u>the Comparative Literature Symposium, Vol. V:</u>
       <u>Modern American Fiction.</u> Wolodymyr T. Zyla and
       Wendell M. Aycock, eds. Lubbock: Texas Tech
       University, 1972, pp. 19-37.

466.   Kazin, Alfred. "The New Realism: SA and Sinclair
       Lewis." <u>On Native Grounds.</u> New York: Reynal
       and Hitchcock, 1942, pp. 205-36.
            Kazin's excellent essay points to Anderson's
       strengths as well as his weaknesses, exposing the tragedy
       of a man who, for the most part, could not capture on paper
       the depth and intensity of his vision. He was hopelessly en-
       snared by "that poignant human situation embodied in him,
       that story he told over and over again because it was his
       only story--of the groping that broke forth out of that search,
       and in the end left all the supplicators brooding, suffering,
       overwhelmed" (217). Anderson did achieve moments of
       greatness in the poignant epiphanies of his best short stories,
       but more importantly, he gave to a younger generation of
       writers "a sense of curiosity, an unashamed acceptance of
       their difficulties and yearnings" (209) that endured long after
       Anderson himself had "come to seem a curiously repetitive
       and even confused figure" (209).

467. Kirchwey, Freda. "SA. " Nation, 152 (22 March
        1941), pp. 313-14.
        Aboard the Panama-bound Santa Lucia in March,
1941, Ms. Kirchwey recalls the final few days of Anderson's
life. Throughout his illness, he maintained an air of opti-
mism and good humor, perhaps not realizing until the last
the seriousness of his condition. Kirchwey says of Anderson, "I can think of no other ambassador to Latin America
who would have expressed more surely and naturally the
characteristics we like to claim for our country--humor and
friendliness and courage and a democratic spirit that is bred
in the bone" (314).

468. Lawry, Jon S. "The Artist in America: The Case
        of SA. " Ball State University Forum, 7 (Spring
        1966), pp. 15-26.
        Lawry finds Anderson a democratic aesthetic
writing essentially for the sake of humanity. The basis for
Anderson's aesthetic is two-fold: 1) he wrote with the cer-
tainty that every person has a humane and idealistic secret
life, a life of the imagination; he was always "interested in
the moment's act when the essence of an imagination lay revealed" (20); and 2) he believed "the artist's imagination is
particularly fitted to receive those revelations" (20-21).
When Anderson coupled his democratic aesthetic with
"proper concern with art for the story's sake" (22), he was
able to produce good fiction. Lawry proceeds to examine
"I Want to Know Why, " "Death in the Woods, " and Many
Marriages in terms of the Andersonian aesthetic tendency.

469. Lewis, Wyndham. "Paleface (12): SA. " The Enemy,
        no. 2 (September 1928), pp. 26-27.
        Lewis says of Anderson: "Of all the children of
Walt Whitman, Sherwood Anderson is perhaps the most cele-
brated; and he has exercised a very great influence upon all
the young school of American fiction, and indeed throughout
the intelligent life of America" (27).

470. Lewisohn, Ludwig. Expression in America. New
        York: Harper's, 1932, pp. 483-88.
        Lewisohn perceives Anderson as the poet and
sayer of the sex-obsessed American. He sees in Anderson
a living John Webster (Many Marriages) driven to the brink
of madness to strange and obscene acts, knocking against
the walls of a stifling life, ever seeking some kind of escape.

471. Lovett, Robert Morss. "SA. " English Journal, 13
        (October 1924), pp. 531-39.

Lovett offers a mid-thirties revaluation of Anderson that perceives Winesburg as Anderson's enduring masterpiece--enlarging his art beyond the limits of naturalism into expressionism--and Dark Laughter as the best of his novels.

473.   McCole, Camille John. "SA--Congenital Freudian."
Catholic World, 130 (November 1929), pp. 129-33.
McCole attacks the Anderson who seems obsessed by the sound of words and in that obsession loses sight of the ideas necessary to productive fiction. He criticizes the Anderson who "blots page after page of his novels with rambling, inchoate, and disconnected thoughts on pigs, epidermis, sex, the birth of children, and the bark of poplar trees" (130). For an understanding of Anderson, McCole turns to Freud. Anderson, like Freud, "is interested primarily in the abnormal" (131), and consequently, he writes of the "day-dreamers, perverts, the 'inhibited,' the morally atrophied, the erotics" (131) and other assorted eccentrics. McCole concludes that "Anderson can never be a great novelist" (133), that he lacks good taste, and that he is a primitive man whose concern with sex is utterly banal.

474.   MacDonald, Dwight. "SA." Yale Literary Magazine,
93 (July 1928), pp. 209-43.

475.   Marble, Annie R. "SA." A Study of the Modern
Novel, British and American, since 1900. New
York: Appleton, 1928, pp. 372-77.
Ms. Marble surveys Andersonian criticism and concludes Anderson "has accumulated much practical knowledge of the seamy side of life and he seeks to unfold these aspects with sincerity and pity" (377).

476.   Marriner, Gerald L. "SA: The Myth of the Artist."
Texas Quarterly, 14 (Spring 1971), pp. 105-16.
Marriner suggests that it was largely through his three autobiographical works that Anderson established the myth of the artist. He examines the relation of the myth to the facts of Anderson's life and then suggests the inner motives for establishing such an elaborate legend. Anderson's own explanation for the myth was that facts were too elusive: "I am a storyteller ... and cannot be expected to tell the truth. Truth is impossible to me." At times, Marriner asserts, "his poetic sensibility led him to alter the facts" (112). Also, a sensitive man, Anderson saw too much frustration and failure in his past to recreate it faithfully and in accurate detail. Finally, Marriner conjectures another rea-

son for Anderson writing of his life as he did: he "did not feel that his life was an isolated example but was rather representative of the artist in America" (114-15).

477. Mather, Frank Jewett. "Anderson and the Institute." Saturday Review of Literature, 23 (5 April 1941), p. 11.
    In a letter to the editor, Mather relates how he secured the assistance of Stuart Sherman and Paul Elmer Ware in sponsoring Anderson's nomination for membership in the National Institute of Arts and Letters. Nominated in 1935, Anderson won the governing board's approval in 1937.

478. Mencken, H. L. "America's Most Distinctive Novelist --SA." Vanity Fair, 27 (December 1926), p. 88.
    Mencken's paragraph of praise is nestled beneath a three-quarters page photograph of Anderson. Mencken finds SA's Dark Laughter "one of the most profound American novels of our time ... a moving and beautiful poem" (88).

479. Michaud, Regis. The American Novel Today. Boston: Little, Brown, 1928, pp. 154-99.
    Michaud devotes two chapters to Anderson, whom he considers a mystic, sensualist, and Freudian writer par excellence. According to Michaud, writing is for Anderson "a groping toward the Unknown, a mystic ejaculation of a mind in quest of itself" (155). Michaud examines Anderson's major works, emphasizing socio-psychological influences and significant autobiographical elements.

480. Miller, Henry. "Anderson the Story-teller." Story, 19 (September-October 1941), pp. 70-74.
    Miller ranks Anderson among the great oral story-tellers he has known, finding him a consummate actor who enriches and enhances the sense of life. In such brilliant stories as "The Egg," Anderson seizes upon "the trivial ... making it important and universal" (72). Perhaps Miller pays SA the highest compliment when he refers to him as a natural story-teller who always gave himself in the fruit of his stories.

481. More, Paul Elmer. The Demon of the Absolute. Princeton: Princeton University Press, 1928, pp. 70-72.
    More finds in A Story Teller's Story a narrative technique of the continuous present: Anderson has "the trick

of beginning again and again and again, and of mixing the
past and the present into a kind of unprogressive circula-
tion" (70).   Of Anderson's treatment of sex in his novels,
More notes, "At the core I should say there was something
wholesome and clean in the author's attitude toward these
matters ... but the idea is lost ... in a drift of morbid
fancies and unclean images that float up unsummoned, and
unrestrained, from the submerged depth of his nature" (71).
In the end, More believes Anderson has failed to utilize his
artistic potential because of an inability to "check the flood
of animal suggestions from his subconscious self" (71).

482.   Morgan, H. Wayne.   "SA: The Search for Unity."
       Writers in Transition: Seven Americans.   New York:
       Hill and Wang, 1963, pp. 82-104.
       Morgan finds in Anderson's work a divided artistic
personality: on the one hand, Anderson "detested the materialism of business; on the other, he clearly saw its potential for good if men would use it in a truly creative way.
Similarly, he was ambivalent in his attitude toward the machine" (85-86), hating it for its displacement of traditional
crafts, but admiring its potential for unification.

483.   Pearson, Norman Holmes.   "Anderson and the New
       Puritanism." Newberry Library Bulletin, Series 2,
       No. 2 (December 1948), pp. 52-63.
       Pearson finds Anderson a leader among the New
Puritans leading the assault on a Puritanism that had de-
clined from its original revolt against conformity and ritual
and had become instead "an unthinking bourgeois morality
without a vital core of feeling and belief" (53).   Rejecting
worn-out values and traditions but optimistically affirming
the rich possibilities of American life, Anderson in his best
writing espouses a "youthful dream which still hopes to pass
through purification to a permanent order of felt beauty and
natural morality" (63).

484.   Phillips, William L.   "SA's Two Prize Pupils."
       University of Chicago Magazine, 47 (January 1955),
       pp. 9-12.   (reprinted in The Achievement of SA.
       Ray Lewis White, ed. Chapel Hill: University of
       North Caroline Press, 1966, pp. 202-10.)
       Phillips provides important information on the
influence of Anderson on Hemingway and Faulkner.   In each
case, Anderson helped the younger writer publish his first
book, influenced the creation of further works through his
own distinctive style and voice, and finally found himself

the subject of hurting literary satire. Phillips places great emphasis on Anderson's role as literary influence: the success of Hemingway and Faulkner, Phillips notes, "is a tribute to the man under whom each worked as an apprentice, and an indication of the lasting debt which we all owe, beyond proper recognition for his own books, to Sherwood Anderson" (12).

485. Quinn, Arthur Hobson. American Fiction, An Historical and Critical Survey. New York: Appleton-Century-Crofts, 1936, pp. 656-60.

In rapid survey fashion, Quinn comments on the bulk of Anderson's novels and short stories and finds much to his dissatisfaction. Windy McPherson's Son is "confused and fumbling in its method" (656); Marching Men descends to "old fashioned melodrama of the purest type" (657); Winesburg deals with characters who are frustrated, lonely, and abnormal, and Quinn asks, "why in the name of sanity and maturity, without which art is sterile, should anyone write about them?" (657); the fumbling and misdirection continues through Many Marriages, where "Anderson went completely mad" (659). Quinn irreverently concludes, the "most astonishing circumstance connected with Sherwood Anderson is the fact that he has been taken seriously" (659).

486. Raymund, Bernard. "The Grammar of Not-reason: SA. " Arizona Quarterly, 12 (Spring-Summer 1956), pp. 136-48.

Raymond discusses the wide range of Anderson's short stories, finding in the best of them a symbolic technique that rivals the best short fiction ever produced in America.

487. Richardson, H. Edward. "Anderson and Faulkner. " American Literature, 36 (November 1964), pp. 299-314.

Richardson points out that Anderson made use of Faulkner in creating the persona David in "A Meeting South. " There are many points of similarity: David's small stature and general features; his love for Keats and Shelley and his being a Southern poet in his own right; David's family background; and his strange appearance because of the bottles of home-brewed spirits carried under his overcoat. More importantly, Richardson notes Anderson's influence on both his early writing and upon the Yoknapatawpha novels. Anderson apparently formed the prototype for Dawson Fairchild in Mosquitoes, and Richardson persuasively argues for Andersonian influence in tone, style, certain rhetorical metaphors and, broadly, in theme. Perhaps, Anderson's greatest gift to Faulkner, however, lay in his championing of the idea of writing of his own life essence. He told Faulkner that a writer "has first got to be what he is, what he is born" (312). Sartoris, appropriately dedicated to Anderson, marks Faulkner's clear understanding of the older writer's message and stands as a highly significant transitional novel in the Faulkner canon.

488.   Richardson, H. Edward. "Faulkner, Anderson, and
        Their Tall Tale." American Literature, 34 (May
        1962), 287-91.
        During the period of their New Orleans friend-
ship, Faulkner and Anderson would walk about the old quarter
of the city and talk. In their conversations, they co-created
fantastic fables of half-horse, half-alligator and later half-
man, half-sheep (and one half-shark) characters--mostly produced for their own entertainment and for the pleasure of
their companions. Richardson points out that Faulkner utilized these tall-tale creations in his second novel, Mosquitoes, thus pointing to a highly credible Andersonian influence.
According to Faulkner's own account, the tales were largely
created by Anderson "with a little help from the younger
writer." (Note: Walter B. Rideout and James B. Meriwether reply to Richardson's article, stating views opposing
the Faulkner-Anderson collaborative effort in the creation of
the tall tales.)

489.   Rideout, Walter B. and Meriwether, James B. "On
        the Collaboration of Faulkner and Anderson." Ameri-
        can Literature, 25 (March 1963), pp. 85-87.
        Responding to H. Edward Richardson's conjecture
that Anderson had largely created the tall tales found in
Faulkner's Mosquitoes, Rideout and Meriwether cite the longer of two letters written by Faulkner to Anderson (contained
in the Anderson collection at the Newberry Library) which
furnishes contradicting evidence. The letter substantiates
that Faulkner played a major role in the creation of the tales
and that he drew upon his own contribution to the Claude
Jackson legend in writing his second novel.

490.   Rideout, Walter B. "Why SA Employed Buck Fever."
        Georgia Review, 13 (Spring 1959), pp. 76-85.
        In November, 1927, Anderson purchased two Vir-
ginia county newspapers, the Marion Democrat and the Smyth
County News. Rideout suggests that editing these papers

helped to alleviate a period of deep depression in Anderson's life. While Anderson wrote most of the newspaper copy himself, he occasionally created additional reporters, the most famous of which is a young mountain man whose genesis Anderson explains: "As I couldn't afford a reporter, I invented one. I call him Buck Fever, a purely mythical being. Buck and I do all the writing." Anderson initiated a fairly regular column entitled "Buck Fever Says" on December 8, 1927. Rideout points out that Anderson used Buck Fever "as a shrewdly humorous reporter of and commentator on current events in Marion and Smyth County" (81). But the importance of Buck goes even further. Rideout argues, "in Anderson's real-life situation Buck was for his creator quite seriously a kind of persona, was, indeed, an actual psychological necessity" (82). To Anderson, Buck must have been a kind of "mask, molded close to the features of his creator, but covering them and allowing him to speak out more completely his complicated feelings toward his position as editor of the newspapers..." (83). Perhaps even more significantly, Buck helped to keep Anderson "brave before the slow, inexorable loss of the storyteller's talent" (85).

491.   Rosenfeld, Paul. Port of New York. New York: Harcourt, 1924, pp. 175-98.

   Rosenfeld holds Anderson in high esteem: "Into the ordered prose of Anderson the delicacy and sweetness of the growing corn, the guttiness and firmness of black earth sifted by the fingers, the broad-breasted power of great laboring horses, has wavered again" (176). While Anderson's "verbal quality was fairly thin" (188) in his first two novels, he completely found his stride in Winesburg and in the best stories of The Triumph of the Egg. Though his range is admittedly limited, "still his stories are the truest, the warmest, the most mature, that have sprung out of the Western soil" (189).

492.   St. John, Donald. "Interview with Hemingway's 'Bill Gorton.'" Connecticut Review, 3 (October 1968), pp. 5-23.

   Essentially a discussion of Bill Smith, on whom Hemingway's Bill Gorton was modeled, the article also recalls Hemingway's meeting with SA in the Chicago apartment of Smith's brother, Y. K. Smith. Anderson seemingly persuaded Hemingway to go to Paris and gave him a letter of introduction to Gertrude Stein.

493.   Samsell, R. L. "Paris Days with Ralph Church."

Fitzgerald-Hemingway Annual (1972), pp. 145-47.
Church, a doctoral candidate at Oxford, became
familiar with the Paris literary crowd (including Hemingway,
Stein, et al.) in the mid-twenties. He had met Hemingway
via a letter of introduction written by Anderson. After Hemingway's parody of Anderson in Torrents of Spring, Church
found himself uncomfortably caught between his two literary
friends. Samsell includes a part of Church's narrative about
those trying times.

494.   Sergel, Roger. "The Man and the Memory." New-
        berry Library Bulletin, Series 2, No. 2 (December
        1948), pp. 44-51.
        Sergel offers a highly personal remembrance of
Anderson that focuses upon intimate, relaxed moments in the
life of a man who "believed that our dreams about each other
are important, perhaps the most important matter of our
lives; that the importance of the man who sits across from
you in the streetcar is above all the dream you have of him,
the past you imagine, the future you project" (45). Anderson's dreams affected not only his fiction, but also his fact.
Sergel cautions scholars who will search through the correspondence at the Newberry: "If they stick to fact, they will
not stick to Anderson. If, for instance, they rely on the
thousands of letters in the Newberry collection, they will rely
on what he wrote in the process of warming up each morning
for his writing. In these, fact and report melt through mood
and conjecture into a fluxion of thought and of the stuff of
dreams" (46). Less seriously, Sergel also remembers the
Anderson who played croquet at Ripshin with such a lust for
winning that games sometimes forced postponement of supper
and ground rules were occasionally shifted to "suit the exi-
gencies of Sherwood's game" (49).

495.   Sinclair, Upton Beall. Money Writes! New York:
        Boni, 1927, pp. 119-23.
        Sinclair refers to Anderson as "muddlement and
nothing else" (119). Upon the basis of data in Anderson's
works, Sinclair psychoanalyzes him and concludes that SA
"is the victim of a dissociated personality" (120). Throughout his life, "the repressed artist in him sobbed and suf-
fered, and lived its own subconscious life" (120) until Anderson, driven to a nervous break-down, rescued the repressed
artistic self and wrote to an audience of critics "whose test
of great literature is that it shall be muddled" (121). Always writing on the same note, all of Anderson's "characters
are victims of dissociation" (121).

496. Smith, Anneliese H. "Part of the Problem, Student
     Responses to SA's 'I Want to Know Why?'" Negro
     American Literature Forum, 7 (1973), pp. 28-31.
          Smith records the response of white students at
     SUNY, Cobbleskill, in 1971-72, to the role of blacks in An-
     derson's story.

497. Smith, Rachel. "SA: Some Entirely Arbitrary Re-
     actions." Sewanee Review, 37 (April 1929), pp. 159-
     63.
          Smith prophesies that Anderson "is undoubtedly
     passing into the dusk which precedes an obliterary darkness"
     (159), and writes as a critic who has tired of the repetitive
     emphasis on isolation and the horrors of the machine age
     which mark Anderson's fiction. While crediting SA with cer-
     tain excellent short stories and appreciating his "telling us
     about the 'wall'" (159), Ms. Smith deplores his attempts at
     the novel and has grown weary of his lack of meaningful mes-
     sage. Smith's article documents a decline in Anderson's
     critical popularity from the unadulterated praise of the early
     twenties.

498. Spencer, Benjamin T. "SA: American Mythopoeist."
     American Literature, 41 (March 1969), pp. 1-18.
          A poet of loneliness and isolation, Anderson
     probed subjectively to the "essence of things." Spencer
     argues that one can trace both Anderson's literary achieve-
     ments and shortcomings to his essential mythopoeic approach
     to American experience. His approach "ran the romantic
     risk of neglecting the existential substance of American ex-
     perience" (16) and often Anderson failed to demonstrate "tight
     syntax, controlled structure, and purified or precise diction"
     (17). However, in the best of his writings, his attention to
     the honest subjective impulse resulted in a penetrating ob-
     servation of the essence of American life, and it is upon the
     power of Anderson's mythopoeic vision that his reputation ul-
     timately shall rest.

499. Stein, Gertrude. "Idem the Same--A Valentine to
     SA." Little Review, 9 (Spring 1923), pp. 5-9.
          Stein offers a free verse poetic valentine to her
     much admired Anderson. The Little Review's "Exile Num-
     ber" includes contributions from Hemingway and e. e. cum-
     mings in addition to Stein and others.

500. Stewart, Maaja A. "Scepticism and Belief in Chekhov
     and Anderson." Studies in Short Fiction, 9 (Winter

1972), pp. 29-40.
Stewart argues a strong affinity between Chekhov and Anderson. Both writers developed a poetic illumination of the most significant inner realities of their characters, and both experienced a strong feeling of cultural failure. Each writer reacted strongly to the void created by his scepticism of the social order, and each created characters who struggle to come to terms with their own vague, inarticulate yearnings. While offering no comprehensive answers to societal problems, Chekhov and Anderson, do, nonetheless, assert an element of human sympathy in the midst of profound scepticism.

501.   Sutton, William A. "SA: The Advertising Years, 1900-1906. " Northwest Ohio Quarterly, 22 (Summer 1950), pp. 120-57.
Sutton discusses in exacting detail the early advertising years in Chicago. Working for Crowell Publishing Company primarily as a copy writer with traveling and solicitation on the side, Anderson received a lucky start when native sagacity combined with pure good fortune. An advertiser had written saying he wanted 200 lines of space in the Crowell magazine. When Anderson arrived to confirm the order, he discovered a great mistake--the man wanted 2000 lines. He wired the man who had hired him, saying: "I have called on my first man.... The order was raised from two hundred to two thousand lines. " Anderson got a sharp raise in pay. Sutton analyzes part of the material Anderson wrote for Agricultural Advertising and The Reader (there are 27 items in the bibliography for this six-year period). Most items appeared in two columns written by Anderson: "Rot and Reason" (1903) and "Business Types" (1904). Each column ran for ten months. Sutton observes that "Rot and Reason" "consisted usually of two or three sketches or essays and was often concluded with a series of five to a dozen epigrams" (124). The material focused on business enterprise and often on agricultural advertising. The ten articles in the "Business Type" series dealt with "typical characters Anderson observed in the course of his activities in the advertising business" (139). They are important, perhaps, because they "represent the first published fruits of his study of his fellow man" (139).

502.   Sutton, William A. "SA: The Cleveland Year, 1906-1907. " Northwest Ohio Quarterly, 22 (Winter 1949-50), pp. 39-44.
The Cleveland year begins on Labor Day, 1906,

when Anderson went to the Ohio City to become president
of the United Factories Company. Anderson was brought
into the firm to inject new blood and revitalize the mail-
order concern through creative, productive advertising (39).
Anderson was to help organize a number of factories into
one group of manufacturers who would peddle their wares together through the "Roofing Catalog" prepared by Anderson.
The firm experienced a shaky year that was highlighted by
the debacle of a faulty line of incubators which involved the
company in a law suit and cost thousands of dollars. In
late summer, 1907, Anderson resigned his presidency and
resolved to enter business on his own.

503. Sutton, William A. "SA: The Clyde Years, 1884-
1896." Northwest Ohio Quarterly, 19 (July 1947), pp.
99-114.
        In his Memoirs Anderson underlines the impor-
tance of the boyhood years in Clyde: "The impressions
gathered by a writer, let us say, in the first twenty years
of his life ... are bound to become source material for him
all his life, and often you have to go far back into childhood
to recapture some of these impressions that become materials." Sutton analyzes the experiences that played upon the
imagination of the artist as a young man. The Andersons
of Clyde, Ohio, were relatively poor, though not destitute
(Anderson tended to play up his poverty even though his
mother "always managed to get materials to make cookies").
Young Sherwood was a diligent worker, earning the nickname
"Jobby" while holding jobs as "newsboy, waterboy, cow-
driver, groom, grocery boy, errand boy, corn-cutter, cab-
bage planter and reaper, worker in a bicycle factory, and
possibly printer's devil" (101). Sherwood spent much time
at the Clyde racetrack and was passionate in his love for
horses, a passion which finds artistic expression in Horses
and Men. Clyde also afforded Anderson an opportunity to
experience first-hand the changes wrought in a country town
by the onslaught of the American industrial revolution.
These experiences, no doubt, influenced Anderson's thinking
in Poor White and in parts of Winesburg, Ohio.

504. Sutton, William A. "SA: The Spanish-American War
Year." Northwest Ohio Quarterly, 20 (January 1948),
pp. 20-36.
        Viewing the Spanish-American War as a "kind of
glamorous national picnic," Anderson enlisted in Company I,
16th Regiment, of the Ohio National Guard and was received
in Clyde as a local hero. As the Company embarked for

regimental headquarters in Toledo, 16 April 1898, Anderson
basked in the sunshine of romantic attention and adventure.
The Company journeyed from Toledo to Camp Bushnell in
Columbus, where Anderson witnessed the brutality of the
volunteers toward those who refused to join the regular army.
Anderson served in the Sixth Ohio Regiment of volunteer infantry from 12 May 1898 until 24 May 1899, having spent
nearly four months in the army base at Cienfuegos, Cuba.
He engaged in no direct fighting.

505. Sutton, William A. "SA's Second Wife." Ball State
      University Forum, 7 (Spring 1966), pp. 39-46.
            In seeking to illuminate the sources of a per-
vasive concern for sexual problems in Anderson's work,
Sutton turns to an examination of his marriage to Tennessee
Mitchell, a woman held in high regard even by Anderson's
first wife Cornelia. Sutton derives his observations of Tennessee from letters and interviews. A remarkable individual, she was interested in music, dance, the theatre, and
eventually became a sculptress. The "Deirdre" of Masters'
Across Spoon River, Tennessee was a woman experienced
in the ways of the world and although she offered Anderson
much love, the loneliness in his life prevented his full ac-
ceptance of her.

506. Tanselle, G. Thomas. "Fitzgerald Letters at New-
      berry." Fitzgerald Newsletter, no. 15 (Fall 1961),
      p. 6.
            In a brief note, Tanselle reviews the Newberry's
three Fitzgerald letters, two of which are to Anderson.
The earlier letter praises SA's Many Marriages; the second
is a brief note alluding to an article on the death of Ring
Lardner.

507. Tanselle, G. Thomas. "Letters of SA and August
      Derleth." Notes and Queries, 12 (July 1965), pp.
      266-73.
            Tanselle publishes for the first time letters ex-
changed between Anderson and Derleth, a Sank City novelist,
between 1939 and 1940. The letters, Tanselle points out,
are significant in that they reflect Anderson's late opinions
(he died less than four months after writing the last letter
to Derleth) "about writers and writing" (266). Further,
"they form a discussion of honesty and freedom in literature
that is eloquent in its own right" (266).

508. Trilling, Lionel. "SA." Kenyon Review, 3 (Sum-

mer 1941), pp. 293-302.

Although Trilling makes adverse judgments on Anderson's works, he is nonetheless haunted by a lingering "residue of admiration" (294). Trilling finds a special poignancy in Anderson's failings, for he perceives that SA set great store in courage, and perhaps not enough in craft. Anderson "had dared too much for art and therefore expected too much from his mere doing, believing that not only fine craft but right opinion must result from it" (295). Perhaps Anderson makes his strongest appeal to "those who read him in adolescence" (295). In stories like "I Want to Know Why" he writes of young people with special tenderness and sensitivity. But the world he creates seems somehow inadequate. Anderson's later writings possess a depressing "compulsive, obsessive quality" (296), and Trilling argues that Anderson's monomania of "love-passion-freedom" (297) eventually made him a grotesque of the kind described in "The Book of the Grotesque." He had taken a vague truth unto himself, called it his truth, and eventually made it into a falsehood. But while Anderson's truth "may have become a falsehood in his hands by reason of limitations in himself ... one has only to take it out of his hands to see again that it is still a truth" (302). Anderson's understanding consciousness of the difficulty of attaining that vague thing he sought constitutes for Trilling "the residue of admiration for him which I find I still have" (302).

509.   Van Doren, Carl. "Revolt from the Village."
        American Novel, 1789-1939. New York: Macmillan,
        1940, pp. 294-302.
        Van Doren interprets Winesburg as a sort of prose Spoon River Anthology with less biting satire and places Anderson's masterpiece squarely amongst those works that focused upon the microcosm of the American village.

510.   Van Doren, Carl. "Sinclair Lewis and SA: A Study
        of Two Moralists." Century, 110 (July 1925), pp.
        362-69.
        Van Doren finds in the writings of Lewis and Anderson strong thematic similarities--both attempt to illustrate the conflict between aspiring individuals and the complacent American society that oppresses them. Their writings particularly reflect an increasing sense of "revolt against the standardized ways of thinking and feeling which have had the approval of the majority" (362) in contemporary America, although each writer approaches this theme in very different ways.

511.   Wagenknecht, Edward Charles. Cavalcade of the
        American Novel. New York: Holt, 1952, pp. 311-
        18.
            Like D. H. Lawrence, Anderson wrote in almost
        every literary genre, but unlike him "he was entirely suc-
        cessful only with his sketches and short stories" (311).
        Wagenknecht proceeds to examine the less successful novels,
        which reflect Anderson's revolt against industrialism, his
        abiding affection for human life, and his near obsession with
        sex.

512.   Walcutt, Charles Child. "SA: Impressionism and
        the Buried Life. " Sewanee Review, 60 (Winter 1952),
        pp. 28-47. (reprinted in his American Literary
        Naturalism, A Divided Stream. Minneapolis: Uni-
        versity of Minnesota Press, 1956, pp. 222-39.)
            Walcutt examines the impact of Anderson's im-
        pressionistic method on Winesburg, Beyond Desire, and Kit
        Brandon. He notes that Anderson explores two major
        themes: discovery and inhibition. The theme of discovery
        relates the "secret insight by which a man's life is suddenly
        revealed to him" (32) (as in "Sophistication" and "The Man
        Who Became a Woman"). The theme of inhibition, present
        in nearly all of Anderson's stories, relates to three broad
        areas of cause and experience: 1) growing up, 2) frustra-
        tion resulting from the absence of a guiding tradition of man-
        ners, and 3) the problem of social opportunity.

513.   Way, Brian. "SA. " The American Novel and the
        Nineteen Twenties. Malcolm Bradbury and David
        Palmer, eds. London: Edward Arnold, 1971, pp.
        106-26.
            Way asserts that Anderson remains one of the
        great masters of the American short story, though he con-
        tributed only a few works of the highest quality. Ander-
        son's reputation must ultimately rest not only on Winesburg,
        but upon such stories as "Unlighted Lamps," "The Sad Horn-
        Blowers, " and "Death in the Woods. " Part II of Way's es-
        say analyzes Winesburg, while Part III offers a concise
        examination of Poor White. Because of the sensitive poetic
        structure that succeeds without impeding narrative flow, Way
        rates "Death in the Woods" Anderson's greatest story.

514.   Weber, Brom. "Anderson and 'The Essence of
        Things. '" Sewanee Review, 59 (Autumn 1951), pp.
        678-92.
            Mr. Weber reviews Andersonian criticism of the

period 1941-1951, lavishing praise on Schevill's notable biography while taking Howe's work on Anderson to task. According to Weber, Howe's approach to Anderson is essentially
wrong: instead of approaching Anderson as a complete critic
with a kind of what-isness sense of inquiry, Howe, like Lionel Trilling, employs "the methodology of a rigid modern
science which knows what it wishes to prove and selects data
which will facilitate its procedure" (683). Howe's dogmatic
zeal results in "a sizable number of minor distortions, mis-
interpretations, and inconsistencies which dubiously lights up
his balance and credibility" (684). In citing the deficiencies
of Howe's work, Weber offers his own penetrating insights
into Anderson's literary career.

515. West, Thomas Reed. "SA: The Machine and the
      Craftsman's Sensibility. " Flesh of Steel: Literature
      and the Machine in American Culture. Nashville:
      Vanderbilt University Press, 1967, pp. 21-34.
      Anderson was particularly susceptible to sensory
perception, and "he urged upon his readers a similar receptivity to existence and to the senses--a receptivity that
he identified with A Story Teller's Story. Anderson's highly
catholic experience of things, his openness to the world of
the senses, led him to distrust constraining societal forces,
such as industrialism and Puritanism. Yet within Anderson's treatment of the coming of industrialism are fully realized characters who stand as "poets of industry" (29) at-
tentively engaged in clean technological creation. Within
their brand of artistry lies an "ice purity" (30) that emphasizes "the frigid tenacity of technological thinking" (30).
Anderson feared the age of industrialism for it spelled the
desolation of all that was beautiful before its advent, but at
the same time he was fascinated by "the delicate complexity
and precision of the modern factory" (34), finding within the
workings of machinery a strange subdued poetic quality.

516. Whipple, Thomas King. "SA. " Spokesmen: Modern
      Writers and American Life. New York: Appleton,
      1928, pp. 115-38.
      Anderson's work has been involved with attempts
"to get beneath the appearances and to understand, by imaginative penetration, the vital processes of American life"
(115). SA lays repeated emphasis on "craftsmanship and
sex ... as means by which man escapes from his personal
cell and joins himself to a larger life and a larger world... "
(136).

517.   White, Ray Lewis, ed. <u>The Achievement of Sherwood</u>
        <u>Anderson: Essays in Criticism.</u> Chapel Hill, North
        <u>Carolina Press, 1966.</u>
            Essays included in Mr. White's collection have
        been listed separately. The Achievement of SA includes
        many of the most significant critical assessments of Ander-
        son and presents a fine balance between favorable and un-
        favorable comment.

518.   White, Ray Lewis. "Introduction." <u>The Achievement</u>
        <u>of SA: Essays in Criticism.</u> Chapel Hill: Univer-
        sity of North Carolina Press, 1966, pp. 3-18.
            Mr. White presents a brilliantly concise over-
        view of Anderson's work and fluctuating literary reputation.
        He examines criticism of Anderson's work and reactions to
        that criticism from the publication of <u>Windy McPherson's</u>
        <u>Son</u> in 1916 to the author's death in 1941. White's analysis
        of criticism reveals an apparent renaissance of interest in
        authors of the period 1900-1940 and partially because of the
        intrinsic reward of studying Anderson himself.

519.   White, Ray Lewis. "Introduction." <u>Return to</u>
        <u>Winesburg: Selections from Four Years of Writing</u>
        <u>for a Country Newspaper.</u> Chapel Hill: University
        of North Carolina Press, 1967, pp. 3-23.
            Mr. White's fascinating introduction traces An-
        derson's yearning desire to return to the life of a small
        town and his ultimate editorship of two country newspapers
        in Marion, Virginia. Though his work often pulled him away
        from Marion and his beloved "Ripshin," Anderson always
        hungered to get home again. He wrote, "There is in the
        life of the small town a possibility of intimacy, a chance to
        know others--an intimacy oftentimes frightening, but which
        can be healing.... There is this narrow but fascinating
        panorama. In a way it is too intimate. Life can never be
        intimate enough" (23). White notes, "In demonstrating the
        essential truth of this paradox lies the value of Sherwood
        Anderson's adventure as a country editor" (23).

520.   White, Ray Lewis. "Introduction." <u>SA/Gertrude</u>
        <u>Stein: Correspondence and Personal Essays.</u> Chapel
        <u>Hill: University of North Carolina Press, 1972, pp.</u>
        3-8.
            Mr. White provides thumbnail sketches of Ander-
        son and Stein, whose childhood experiences and educational
        backgrounds stand in striking contrast, and he describes
        their chance meeting (see Sylvia Beach, no. 385) in Paris
        in June, 1921.

521. White, Ray Lewis. "SA's First Published Story. "
Readers and Writers, 1 (April 1968), pp. 32-38.

522. White, Ray Lewis. article in The Politics, pp. 251-
62. 1971.

523. Woolf, Virginia. "American Fiction. " Saturday Review of Literature, 2 (1 August 1925), pp. 1-3.
According to Ms. Woolf, of all American novel-
ists the most discussed and read in England in 1925 were
Anderson and Sinclair Lewis. Ms. Woolf discusses these
two authors in terms of their distinct Americanness. She
finds Anderson powerfully crude and simple, a fit successor
to Walt Whitman, and she praises The Triumph of the Egg,
for in that collection of stories Anderson bored beneath the
surface to the "deeper and warmer layer of human nature"
(2).

524. Wright, Austin M. The American Short Story in the
Twenties. Chicago: University of Chicago Press,
1961, pp. 2-3, 11, 14-16, 18, 21, 26ff.
Wright's book constitutes a critical-historical
survey and tribute to five American authors of the 1920's--
Anderson, Fitzgerald, Hemingway, Faulkner, and Porter--
"who perfected the forms of the modern short story in
America" (2). Wright discusses stories in each of Anderson's major collections of short stories.

2. Individual Works and Collections

Beyond Desire

525. Rideout, Walter B. "Introduction. " Beyond Desire.
New York: Liveright, 1961, pp. vii-xiii.
Rideout's Introduction emphasizes that Beyond
Desire is more than one of the strike novels of the "Angry
Thirties": "What Anderson is really concerned with is the
effect of industrialism, not only on workers, but on the
whole human community in microcosm" (viii). Anderson's
concern with industrialism had earlier surfaced in Poor
White (and to a lesser intensity in Winesburg). Rideout sees
Red Oliver as "The most important person in the book" (x),

for in the midst of confusion and chaos he dares to question
life.   While Beyond Desire remains an essentially uneven
work, Anderson is at his best in Book Two, "Mill Girls,"
and Rideout's overview of the novel concurs with Anderson's
own verdict: "I knew well enough that the book is sound,
and I believe it will take its definite place in the story of
our American civilization..." (xiii).

(Further references: 375, 376, 377, 379, 380, 382, 421,
446, 456, 460, 462, 463, 498, 508, 518.)

Dark Laughter

526.   Krutch, Joseph Wood. "Vagabonds." American
        Criticism, 1926. New York: Harcourt, 1926, pp.
        108-11.

527.   Lovett, Robert Morss. "SA, American." Virginia
        Quarterly Review, 17 (Summer 1941), pp. 379-88.
        Lovett suggests Anderson's own story might be
titled "The Education of SA" and "put forth as an account of
the curriculum of life as opposed to that of the schools"
(381).   Anderson's education was directed toward the making
of an American artist, and during that education he learned
to appreciate "the distorted and incongruous elements of life,
at once humorous and sympathetic" (388).   Lovett puts forth
Dark Laughter as containing "all the distinguishing notes of
Anderson's fiction" (386).   More than in any earlier novel,
Anderson achieves "an artistic unity through a clearer view
and a stronger, more persistent grasp of his material and
its meaning.   That material is, as always, experience and
its meaning is in the contrast between the logic of events,
of an actual situation, and that of intellectual discrimination
and classification" (386).

528.   McHaney, Thomas L. "Anderson, Hemingway, and
        Faulkner's The Wild Palms." PMLA, 87 (May 1972),
        pp. 465-74.
        McHaney's fascinating article demonstrates how
Faulkner's The Wild Palms reveals "basic differences be-
tween Faulkner and Hemingway regarding the nature of hu-
man and fictional reality and indicates agreement between
Faulkner and Anderson" (465).   Both The Wild Palms and
Mosquitoes bear strong thematic resemblance to Anderson's
Dark Laughter; in each instance, the "restraints of a puri-
tanical morality and the pressures of materialism destroy

art as well as love" (466). McHaney also presents strong
extrinsic evidence which suggests Tennessee Mitchell Anderson may have been Faulkner's original for the heroine of
The Wild Palms. For Faulkner to have created such a detailed and accurate resemblance, he must have learned much
about Tennessee through Sherwood.

529. Sherman, Stuart P. Critical Woodcuts. New York:
      Scribner's, 1926, pp. 3-17.
      Sherman finds in Dark Laughter an economy, an
intensity, and a poignant reality comparable in craftmanship
to Pride and Prejudice. He appreciates Anderson's symbolic method, his ear for the "idiom of American colloquial
speech" (11), his deep-rooted Americanness, his story-telling
powers, and his elemental mysticism.

530. Tugwell, Rexford Guy. "An Economist Reads Dark
      Laughter." New Republic, 45 (9 December 1925), pp.
      87-88.
      An essentially sympathetic analysis of Dark
Laughter, Tugwell's essay focuses upon Bruce Dudley as
representative of the modern man who will not be bribed by
the pleasures the machine age offers to men to make them
do the work against which they naturally rebel. Tugwell
notes in mock horror: "This man Bruce Dudley threatens
to tear apart the careful veiling we have wound about our
heads, to muffle ears and blur eyes" (88). Through Dudley,
Anderson threatens to make us see.

531. White, Ray Lewis. "Hemingway's Private Explanation
      of The Torrents of Spring." Modern Fiction Studies,
      13 (Summer 1967), pp. 261-63.
      Mr. White analyzes five letters from Hemingway
to Anderson in which Hemingway shows concern for the pain
his satire of Dark Laughter may have caused Anderson, but
in which Hemingway also affirms his right and duty as an
artist to criticize what he considered sloppy, sentimental
writing. Should an artist refrain from such criticism, he
can in no way help the originator of the work develop his
writing skills. Hemingway apparently believed that writers,
among themselves, should have to pull no punches.

532. Wickham, Harvey. "Laughter and SA." The Impuri-
      tans. New York: L. MacVeagh, 1929, pp. 268-82.
      Wickham examines Windy McPherson's Son and
Tar enroute to criticizing Dark Laughter, a novel that points
to something wrong in American society. Anderson echoes

the dark laughter, and "civilization is the butt of the joke"
(282). But Wickham must ask whether Anderson has really
"put his hand upon the cancer?" (282).

(Further references: 375, 376, 377, 379, 380, 382, 423,
427, 435, 443, 452, 453, 456, 457, 460, 461, 462, 463,
464, 466, 472, 475, 478, 479, 485, 493, 498, 508, 509,
511, 515, 516, 518.)

Death in the Woods

533.   Bland, Winifred. "Through a College Window."
        Story, 19 (September-October 1941), pp. 82-86.
            In Story's special issue Bland reprints her re-
view of "Death in the Woods." Each of the sixteen stories
comprises a sort of vivisection of life, and Bland finds four
of them particularly striking: "There She Is--She is Taking
Her Bath," "A Meeting South," "Brother Death," and "In a
New Strange Town." She concludes that Anderson's "position
as a novelist might remain in doubt, but as a short story
writer he has achieved his place in the sun" (86).

534.   Guerin, Wilfred L. "'Death in the Woods:' SA's
        'Cold Pastoral.'" CEA Critic, 30 (May 1968), pp.
        4-5.
            Guerin places "Death in the Woods" with Keats'
sonnets on the sonnet and Pirandello's Six Characters in
Search of an Author as "literature written about literature"
(4). The narrator in the story knows that he is trying to
tell a story. What then is the real story? Guerin suggests
there are several levels to the total story: 1) the archetype
of imitation; 2) the feeding of life; but most importantly, 3)
the story through its telling becomes an art object, "the end
result of formative processes that take place largely in the
unconscious, aided by conscious memory" (5). If the artist
relates more than he himself knows, it is because he "car-
ries within himself the gun and the sum total of everything
important about his art product" (5).

535.   Joselyn, Sister Mary, O.S.B. "Some Artistic Di-
        mensions of SA's 'Death in the Woods.'" Studies in
        Short Fiction, 4 (Spring 1967), pp. 252-59.
            Sister Joselyn suggests that "Death in the Woods"
is "built upon at least four transformations" (253): 1) that
of Mrs. Grimes--"from girl to woman, feeder, and victim,

then to the perceptual, 'frozen' embodiment of the young
girl caught in 'marble'" (255); 2) that of the young narrator
--completion of his sense of self through the expression of
the woman's story as a work of art; 3) that of the seven
dogs into wolves--a metamorphosis that remains incomplete
in the eyes of the narrator; and 4) the alteration of the material facts of the story into a work of art. Through the in-
terlocking of these transformations, SA creates a perfectly
integrated art form.

536. Lawry, Jon S. "'Death in the Woods' and the Art-
     ist's Self in SA. " PMLA, 74 (June 1959), pp. 306-
     11.
         Lawry argues that "Death in the Woods" is con-
cerned not only with Mrs. Grimes, but with the "receiving
(here, a creating) consciousness--the 'I' of the story" (307).
The two lives converge, "culminating in the sense of revelation the narrator feels in seeing the unknown woman's body,
perfected in death, which permits him to see the young
woman and, beyond her, the freed human being behind the
anonymous thing called 'Mrs. Grimes'" (307). The narrator
progresses from "blank observation of historical fragments,
through pity, to whole knowledge" (307). The narrator's
discovery of a sense of self necessarily involved artistic expression of the story of the woman. The narrator pierces
the mask of surface reality and gleans the essence of human
experience beneath. His vision dramatizes Anderson's belief
that the artist discovers the essence of human existence only
through surrender of self-concern. The concept of self is
closely akin to imagination or fancy, which for Anderson
"stand always for the opposite of fact, and are the sole
agents of truth about men" (309). In "Death in the Woods"
the male "narrator surrenders self, only to gain it. By his
imagination and creative communion with the woman--by discovering her--he discovers a greater reality within himself"
(311).

537. Miller, William V. "The Death in the Forest. "
     Tar: A Midwest Childhood, A Critical Text. Ray
     Lewis White, ed. Cleveland, Ohio: Press of Case
     Western Reserve University, 1969, pp. 231-36.
         Miller edits a twenty-two page holograph, located
in the Anderson Collection at the Newberry Library, which
is an early draft, though probably not a first draft, of
"Death in the Woods. "

538. Robinson, Eleanor M. "A Study of 'Death in the

Woods. '" CEA Critic, 30 (January 1968), p. 6.
    Ms. Robinson argues that "Death in the Woods"
accomplishes two things simultaneously: 1) it relates the
tragic story of a woman born to singular purpose--feeding
life; and 2) it attempts to explain the process of narration.
In contrast to Chekhovian short story technique, Anderson
"shows us the author through a long time span looking back
at a specific event in the past" (6). Robinson suggests that
"all narration is written as the process is described in the
Anderson story" (6). An event happens; it is perceived but
not immediately understood; still, it grates at the active consciousness until it begins to make sense; then the artist
pieces together the reality of the experience with the workings of his imagination.

539.   Rohrberger, Mary. "The Man, the Boy, and the
        Myth: SA's 'Death in the Woods.'" Midcontinent
        American Studies Journal, 3 (Fall 1962), pp. 48-54.
            Ms. Rohrberger interprets the symbolism of
"Death in the Woods" in terms of the Demeter-Proserpine-
Hecate myth. In her symbolic function as nourisher, Mrs.
Grimes may be seen as a Demeter figure; the "figure of
Proserpine can be identified with the young woman who, on
a June day at the wheat harvest, is carried away by Jake
Grimes in a horse and buggy amid much violence" (52); the
identification with Hecate is accomplished as the old woman
dies with the moon coming out and dogs howling--"Hecate
symbolizes the essential female governed by the moon" (53).
The boy who observes the material events of the story is
unable to understand what he has experienced; "as a man he
feels compelled to tell the story in the hope of understanding,
but he remains dissatisfied" (53). In relating Anderson's
tale to ancient myths of rebirth and regeneration, Ms. Rohrberger identifies a continuing history of literary attempts to
understand the mysteries of life and death.

(Further references: 375, 376, 377, 379, 380, 382, 420,
425, 435, 447, 468, 478, 482, 483, 486, 498, 509, 513,
518, 524.)

Hello Towns!

540.   Anderson, David D. "SA, Virginia Journalist. "
        Newberry Library Bulletin, 6 (July 1971), pp. 251-52.
            David D. Anderson persuasively argues that Hello

Towns! is far more than a mere collection of Marion, Virginia news items and sketches. Organized to represent a year in the life of both Anderson and the town, the book aesthetically "reproduces the cyclical basis of all life, including that of a community. The material is not tied artificially together; instead each part of it occurs as spontaneously as do the events of life itself" (259). In Anderson's able hands, country journalism transcends traditional reportage and achieves a kind of literary craftsmanship that penetrates to the essence of Southern small-town life. Anderson's experience as townsman and editor helped him to become as familiar with Marion Virginians as he had been with Midwesterners of Clyde, Ohio. Through Hello Towns! Anderson was subconsciously moving toward Beyond Desire, Kit Brandon, and his other records of the impact of industrialism on the individual in the South" (255).

(Further references: 375, 376, 377, 379, 380, 382, 420, 518.)

Horses and Men

541. Babb, Howard S. "A Reading of SA's 'The Man Who Became a Woman.'" PMLA, 80 (September 1965), pp. 432-35.
      While not denying that homosexuality is a major motif in "The Man Who Became a Woman," Babb argues that Anderson is concerned with something more: a particular integrity of being that Herman Dudley must experience as a requisite for maturing. In basic outline, the story records Dudley's 'progress from a conventional existence through a series of fantastic episodes in which he reveals an integrity of being--a responsiveness to every kind of experience--that qualifies him for growing up, for coming to some terms with conventional life" (434).

542. Lucow, Ben. "Mature Identity in SA's 'The Sad Horn-Blowers.'" Studies in Short Fiction, 2 (Spring 1965), pp. 291-93.
      Lucow argues that the mournful cornet playing of Tom Appleton and the unnamed old man are inseparably tied to the "story's theme of the difficulty or impossibility, of growing up into identifiable manhood in Will Appleton's world" (293). But also, their playing constitutes an act of rebellion, an almost tragi-comic assertion of their human

presence in a world which seeks to equate mature identity
with "absorption into a homogeneous mass" (293).

(Further references: 375, 376, 377, 379, 380, 382, 420,
432, 433, 434, 435, 446, 448, 453, 456, 458, 463, 466,
471, 475, 482, 485, 486, 509, 513, 516, 518, 524.)

Kit Brandon

543.   Sergel, Roger. "Of SA and Kit Brandon." Book
        Buyer, Series r, v. 2, No. 7 (November 1936), pp.
        2-4.
        Appraising Kit Brandon as Anderson's "best novel,
and by any standard, a great novel" (2), Sergel nonetheless
finds an occasional "uncouthness about Anderson's style" (4).
The occasional flaws hardly mar an otherwise adroit, powerful work that finds "in the America of prohibition days and
nights, the lawless and violent heart of America" (4).   In
the end, when Kit leaves, revolted by the violence, she significantly sets forth to seek, not money, but a partnership
in living.   Sergel suggests that when Anderson went up into
the Virginia mountains, he "must have heard voices in the
laurel bushes, for he has come down out of the mountains
with a book of revelation" (4).

544.   Taylor, Welford D. "Kit Brandon A Reidentifica-
        tion." Newberry Library Bulletin, 6 (July 1971), pp.
        263-67.
        Taylor argues that Mrs. Willie Carter Sharpe,
rather than Ms. Mamie Palmer (see White, no. 547), was
Anderson's original for the heroine of Kit Brandon.   Taylor's theory is based upon certain public utterances made by
Anderson in "Man and His Imagination" and upon evidence
contained in a recently discovered scrapbook in which Anderson supposedly collected materials for his last novel.
Parallels between Mrs. Sharpe and Kit are many: both
worked in five-and-dime stores; both quit their jobs to mar-
ry sons of prominent bootleggers; both wore a shiny dental
diamond; both enjoyed fast cars; and they had similar modus
operandi for their illegal rum-running.

545.   Taylor, Welford. "SA." Virginia Cavalcade, 19
        (Spring 1970), pp. 42-47.
        Taylor recalls Anderson's stay in Virginia--a
tenure "beneficial to both the man and the commonwealth"

(42). He suggests that in Kit Brandon Anderson "most clearly reflects his Virginia experience" (47) and in the microcosm of his southern world makes a fitting statement about the nation as a whole--all men should live with the harmony SA experienced in Southwest Virginia.

546. Van Doren, Mark. "Still Groping." Private Reader. New York: Holt, 1942, pp. 247-51.
    Van Doren offers a scathing review of Kit Brandon, likening Anderson more to a baby groping than an artist writing purposely with a story to tell. Kit Brandon and Tim Halsey are, in Van Doren's mind, just warmed-over versions of previous Anderson protagonists.

547. White, Ray Lewis. "The Original for SA's Kit Brandon." Newberry Library Bulletin, 6 (December 1965), pp. 196-99.
    White examines stories from the Smyth County News that reveal obvious parallels between the lives of the real Mamie Palmer, bootlegging queen, and the fictious Kit Brandon, and thus suggests that Mamie Palmer may have been the original for Anderson's heroine.

548. Williams, Cratis D. "Kit Brandon, A Reappraisal." Shenandoah, 13 (Spring 1962), pp. 55-61.
    Williams attempts to resurrect Kit Brandon from undeserved critical neglect. He points to the novel's unity in fusion of materials, style, and technique and to Anderson's integrity as a writer in making mountain girls, hillbillies, and moonshiners integrally appropriate to the demands of art.

(Further references: 375, 376, 377, 379, 380, 381, 420, 435, 456, 466, 480, 498, 508, 511, 518.)

Many Marriages

549. Collins, Joseph. "Sophism and SA." Taking the Literary Pulse. New York: George H. Doran Company, 1924, pp. 29-47.
    Collins sees Anderson as a product of his heredity and environment: "His heredity is Puritanic, his environment the Middle West. He deludes himself with the belief that he has escaped the tentacles of the former, and he plumes himself that the furnishings of the latter have

given him the right to prophetic utterance about future
America and Americans" (29). Anderson heads the American
literary school of "sex-obsession" (30). The bulk of Collins'
psychological criticism falls upon Many Marriages where Anderson "has sailed his bark, freighted with a soul in search
of release from its own futility and realization of its vague
yearnings for godship, unto the troubled waters of a sea of
symbolism and mysticism" (38).

550.   Wilson, Edmund. "Many Marriages." Dial, 74
        (April 1923), pp. 399-400.
            Although he finds Many Marriages "tedious and
sometimes flat" (399) and the characters--especially Mrs.
Webster--nearly "stripped of their personalities" (399), Wilson is yet "disturbed and soothed by the feeling of hands
thrust down among the deepest bowels of life--hands delicate
and clean but still pitiless in their explorations" (400). If
Anderson has produced a feeble, even flabby, novel, he has
nonetheless retained a sense of integrity in the "pursuit of
his own authentic ideal" (400). He has not failed from an
attempt to imitate the ideals of others.

(Further references: 375, 376, 377, 379, 380, 382, 427,
433, 434, 435, 446, 448, 452, 456, 457, 460, 462, 463,
464, 468, 470, 471, 472, 479, 485, 508, 510, 511, 515,
516, 518.)

                            Marching Men

551.   Hackett, Francis. "To American Workingmen."
        Horizons. New York: Huebsch, 1918, pp. 57-61.
        (reprinted in The Achievements of SA. Ray Lewis
        White, ed. Chapel Hill: University of North Caro-
        lina Press, 1966, pp. 26-29.)
            Proclaiming Marching Men a "proletarian novel"
(58), Francis Hackett is quick to point out serious weaknesses: the making of McGregor into a primordial hero
figure, the near ludicrousness of the scheme by which a
Pennsylvania miner aspires to evoke solidarity of labor.
However, there is a living presence in the novel, an accurate and sensitive vision that saves it from critical damnation: one experiences a "freshness of feeling about workingmen and women, the vividly frank and abrupt opinions, the
flashes of energetic description, ... the details of mining-
town and apple-warehouse and night restaurant and Chicago

pulchritude, the reminiscence of 1893 and of First Ward
infamies, the swiftness of incident" (58).

552. White, Ray Lewis. "Introduction." Marching Men,
     A Critical Text. Cleveland and London: Press of
     Case Western Reserve University, 1972, pp. xi-xxvii.
     White's critical edition of Marching Men is not
identical to either Anderson's penultimate manuscript or the
first printed book, but rather comprises a "cautious recon-
struction of Sherwood Anderson's valid manuscript readings
along with clearly marked incorporation of major substantives
from the printed version of the novel" (xxvii). White's introduction provides fascinating background information on the
writing of Marching Men and explains at length the difficulties inherent in attempting to edit a major Anderson volume.
Mr. White also reprints a selection of Anderson's earliest
published essays and short fiction (from the period 1902-
1914), "documents of considerable importance to the reader
interested in the transformation of a middle-ages Ohio businessman into the author of Winesburg, Ohio" (xxvii).

(Further references: 375, 376, 377, 378, 380, 382, 405,
424, 433, 434, 435, 438, 444, 450, 452, 456, 457, 460,
464, 466, 471, 475, 479, 482, 483, 485, 491, 495, 508,
509, 510, 511, 515, 516, 518, 594, 606.)

Mid-American Chants

553. Ford, Thomas. "The American Rhythm: Mary Aus-
     tin's Poetic Principle." Western American Litera-
     ture, 5 (1970), pp. 3-14.
     Ford notes that Mary Austin believed Anderson,
Sandburg, and Vachel Lindsay occasionally succeeded in capturing natural American rhythms in their poetry (in contrast
to early American Puritan writers like Lowell and Longfel-
low who were influenced by classic models). Ford compares
stanzas from poems in Mid-American Chants to Pawnee ritual poetry, noting that in both "the earth, the corn is the
source of strength, wisdom, life; and is, in fact, a goddess"
(7). Both have an unaccented pyrrhic meter, and both are
unrhymed. Anderson's poetry resembles that of the Amerind,
though records of this movement were not available for Anderson to imitate.

554. Rideout, Walter B. "SA's Mid-American Chants."

Aspects of American Poetry: Essays Presented to
Howard Mumford Jones. Richard M. Ludwig, ed.
Columbus: Ohio State University Press, 1962, pp.
149-70.

Rideout justifies a careful examination of Mid-
American Chants because it may provide "insights into both
man and writer" (150) and demonstrate that Anderson's "life
and work are reciprocally illuminating" (150). The work has
probably received its critical due, for "Anderson was a better poet in prose than in verse, despite his feelings that the
poems were among the most intimate expressions of his inner life" (149). The poems that comprise Mid-American
Chants were written in one creative burst of energy from
late February, 1917, to mid-April or possibly May of that
year. Rideout suggests the influence of Whitman may be
seen in "the long, unrhymed lines; the rhetorical rhythms
with their balanced elements and repetitions, even brief
catalogues of states, cities, rivers" (158). Of the imagery
that abounds in the Chants, the most significant is the imagery of cornfields, the symmetry of which "suggests that
order had an obsessive value for Anderson" (169). Rideout
points to external evidence which suggests the notion that
the need to find an order was compelling for Anderson--a
compulsion which later led to his first novel, Poor White.

(Further references: 375, 376, 377, 379, 380, 382, 405,
427, 433, 444, 452, 471, 478, 483, 498, 518, 606.)

New Testament

555.   Aiken, Conrad. A Reviewer's ABC. New York:
        Meridian Books, 1958, pp. 130-32.
        In A Reviewer's ABC, Conrad Aiken gathers to-
gether the accumulated critical work of nearly half a century. He offers only faint praise of the "free verse symbolism, or poetic prose or parable, or whatever one wants
to call it" (131) of Anderson's A New Testament. Overall,
he finds Anderson's symbolisms "too wholesale to be effective, too amorphous to be clear, too structureless and hu-
morless to be anything more than readable" (132).

(Further references: 375, 376, 377, 379, 381, 382, 391,
518.)

Plays: Winesburg and Others

556. Wentz, John C. "Anderson's Winesburg and the
      Hedgerow Theatre. " MD, 3 (May 1960), pp. 42-51.
      Wentz records the history of the dramatized ver-
sion of Winesburg. Anderson had first become interested in
revising Winesburg for the stage in 1919, when Jacques Co-
peau, head of the Vieux Columbier acting troupe, suggested
to Anderson the book's rich theatre possibilities. However,
Anderson did not seriously undertake the task of rewriting
until 1933, after Arthur Barton had authored an unsatisfactory version. Whartron Esherick, a sculptor and long-time
friend, convinced Jasper Deeter, director of the Hedgerow
Theatre, to produce the play. On 30 June 1934, Winesburg,
Ohio was presented to a capacity (167 seats) crowd who enjoyed the play tremendously, although certain objections were
later raised on moral grounds. Active in repertory for three
years, Winesburg was performed forty-one times and grossed
$3,352.41, thus achieving an average record at Hedgerow.

(Further references: 375, 376, 377, 379, 380, 382.)

Poor White

557. Anderson, David D. "SA's Larger View. " Critical
      Studies in American Literature: A Collection of Es-
      says. Karachi, Pakistan: University of Karachi,
      1964, pp. 132-41.
      SA wrote in the introduction to the Modern Li-
brary edition of Poor White that his novel was in some ways
an autobiography of a town in the midst of its transition
from agrarian to industrial economy. David D. Anderson
cautions against taking this notion too literally, for Poor
White is "in fact not the biography of a town but the biography of people in the town whose lives have been warped
by industrialism and its concomitant greed" (133). As in
Winesburg, SA focuses his attentions upon individual lives,
but use of the novel form allows more detailed concentration
on fewer characters. Anderson outlines SA's indebtedness
to Mark Twain and to the Lincoln legend in creation of the
novel's major characters and distinct midwest American
background. While Poor White remains significant for its
recording of the effects of industrialism upon the small
town, it is structurally flawed by interruptive digressions

and an indecisive conclusion. It remains, however, superior
to Anderson's earlier novels largely because SA was able to
recapture the "natural idioms and rhythms of Winesburg,
Ohio" (140).

558.   Gelfant, Blanche Housman. "SA, Edith Wharton, and
        Thomas Wolfe." The American City Novel. Norman:
        University of Oklahoma Press, 1954, pp. 95-132.
        Gelfant perceives the central achievement of Poor
White as a historical dramatization of the transition of the
small town (Bidwell) in America into a modern industrialized
urban community. The novel's central character, Hugh Mc-
Vey, is identified with the process of urbanization, and the
larger collapse of the agrarian community is "represented
through the gallery of townspeople, all of whom undergo a
change as Bidwell becomes industrialized" (101). In the sub-
plot surrounding harness-maker Jim Wainsworth, Anderson
dramatizes the conflict between craftsmanship and the machine
age. As Wainsworth is gradually displaced, "the personal
rewards of craftsmanship--integrity, independence, pride,
self-respect, and honesty--are also disappearing" (103). A
second major theme attendant to the rise of industrialism is
the failure of love, most poignantly embodied in the unsuc-
cessful marriage of Hugh and Clara.

559.   Hoffman, Frederick John. The Twenties. New York:
        Viking, 1955, pp. 302-306 and passim.
        Hoffman's book analyzes American writing in the
twenties. A central part of the chapter, "Science and the
'Precious Object,'" examines Poor White as one of the important novels which addressed the problem of the machine
age, and more broadly, the complex problems of industrialism. Hoffman writes, "Anderson did not deny the industrial
age, but he regretted its influence in destroying the 'poetry
and vague thoughts' available to a pre-industrial sensibility"
(306).

560.   Rideout, Walter B. "Introduction." Poor White.
        New York: Viking, 1966, pp. ix-xx.
        Rideout points out that Anderson's attack on in-
dustrialism in Poor White is threefold: 1) industrialism dis-
regards the aesthetic--the factories produce noise and sun-
obscuring smoke as well as manufactured goods; 2) it dis-
places traditional craftsmanship; and 3) overemphasis on
money-making perverts human relationships and individuals
themselves (xvii). Contemporary readers of Poor White experience a kind of nostalgia that reinforces our notion that

modern industrialism is a curse as well as a blessing. Anderson's novel accurately records the passing of an age that seems almost idyllic in its agrarian simplicity.

(Further references: 375, 376, 377, 379, 380, 382, 423, 433, 434, 435, 438, 448, 453, 454, 460, 462, 463, 466, 471, 472, 475, 479, 482, 495, 498, 509, 510, 511, 513, 515, 516, 518, 628.)

Story Teller's Story

561. Beach, Joseph Warren. The Outlook for American Prose. Chicago: University of Chicago Press, 1926, pp. 247-80.

Beach appreciates A Story Teller's Story because it captures the essence of something distinctly American, and it does so, not through a vocabulary of intellectual abstraction but through clear and simple speech patterns that belie a highly sensitive human consciousness. Anderson's "natural instinct, his mental process, lends itself to a syntax almost as simple as that of the Bible" (252. In A Story Teller's Story, Beach observes "an open, flowing rhythm, as of one writing easily, without cramp and tension, such as it is hard to match in our prose" (256).

562. Lewis, Sinclair. "A Pilgrim's Progress." The Man from Main Street; a Sinclair Lewis Reader. New York: Random House, 1953, pp. 165-68.

Valuable for its insights into the literary mind of Sinclair Lewis as well as the literary merits of A Story Teller's Story, "A Pilgrim's Progress" argues against those critics who would find in Anderson no sense of humor and a morbid preoccupation with sex. Lewis notes no sex obsession and finds humor in plenty, "humor equally free of the hysterical vulgarity of the Bill Nye school and the neat little jabs of contemporary New York wit" (167). Aside from the book's intimate and candid revelation of a genuine craftsman, it offers also an engaging explanation of the emerging Middle West and a stream of cornbelt characters who are as "significant and beautiful as any Russian peasant, any naughty French countess, any English vicar, any tiresomely familiar dummy of standard fiction" (168). (Note: article originally published as a review in the 9 November 1924 issue of the New York Tribune Books.)

563.   Rideout, Walter B.   "Preface."   A Story Teller's
        Story.   New York: Viking, 1969.
            In introducing A Story Teller's Story, Rideout
points out that the first edition in 1924 received generally
favorable reviews and was moderately popular.   Critics in
the thirties and forties, however, found the autobiographical
facts unreliable and claimed the book was structurally dis-
organized.   Rideout argues that in the first place, Anderson
never meant to create a factual autobiography, but rather
sought to penetrate the surface reality to explore imaginatively the essence of his own buried existence.   Secondly, the
book is very carefully structured: "Each of the four 'Books'
is organized around contrasting themes--fact opposed to fancy in Book One, love turned inward on the self (Judge Turner) opposed to love turned outward on others (Alonzo Berners)
in Book Two, the demands of business opposed to the demands of art in Book Three, the search for identity and
community of the Midwest artist as opposed to the culture
of the American East and of Europe in Book Four."   Each
Book further culminates in a symbolic summary of the state
of chronological, imaginative development of the artist as he
progresses through the book, and an epilogue poses the final
challenge--"Whether the American writer has the courage to
create art out of his honest reaction to native materials."

564.   Tanselle, G. Thomas.   "Anderson Annotated by
        Brooks."   Notes and Queries, 15, No. 2 (February
        1968), pp. 60-61.
            Tanselle describes annotations made by Van Wyck
Brooks in personal copies of Perhaps Women and A Story
Teller's Story.   Underlining and marginal notes are most ex-
tensive in the latter book.   The interested reader can, by
checking the pages listed by Tanselle, "see what passages
struck Brooks most when he read A Story Teller's Story"
(61).

(Further references: 375, 376, 377, 379, 380, 382, 423,
427, 433, 435, 445, 446, 447, 448, 456, 460, 461, 462,
463, 466, 472, 476, 485, 486, 495, 498, 508, 509, 510,
513, 515, 516, 518, 523, 628.)

                Tar: A Midwest Childhood

565.   Anderson, David D.   "Emerging Awareness in SA's
        'Tar.'"   Ohioana, 4 (Summer 1961), pp. 40-41, 51.

Admitting that many of Anderson's works were essentially autobiographical, David D. Anderson argues that SA was more concerned with recording feelings than facts. Thus, one must view Anderson's works as a "multi-volumed spiritual biography that sets forth the record of generic man in the unique period that saw America transformed from an agricultural to an industrial state' (40-41). Tar: A Midwest Childhood, a significant volume in SA's spiritual biography, represents the author's attempt to examine the "earliest experiences of man in an America suddenly conscious of its industrial and commercial potential" (42). Through Tar, Anderson analyzes "man's loss of innocence and freedom as a practical society emerges around him" (42), a theme that surfaces time and again in Anderson's work.

566. Sutton, William A. "The Diaries of SA's Parents. " Tar: A Midwest Childhood, A Critical Text. Ray Lewis White, ed. Cleveland: Press of Case Western Reserve University, 1969, pp. 219-30.
Sutton's editing of the diaries of Anderson's parents' diaries for the critical edition of Tar reveals a mother (Emma Smith Anderson) who seems quite satisfied with her busy, if limited, life in Camden, Ohio, and a father (Irwin Anderson) who appears to have been a harder worker and more religiously faithful than his fictional counterpart in Tar.

567. West, Rebecca. "SA, Poet. " Strange Necessity. Garden City: Doubleday, Doran, 1928, pp. 309-20.
Ms. West ranges wide in her observations of Anderson's work, but the bulk of her comments rest on Tar, a work marred by unevenness and "sham naivete" (318), but one which nevertheless contains flourishes of genius. She finds SA important in the contemporary field of American writers because of his poetic bent and the "vein of authentic inspiration" (320) underlying his works.

568. White, Ray Lewis. "Introduction. " Tar: A Midwest Childhood, A Critical Text. Cleveland: Press of Case Western Reserve University, 1969, pp. xi-xx.
White points out that Tar is essentially an imaginative recreation of Anderson's childhood years from 1876 to 1895. In the semi-fictional memoir, Tar, "young Sherwood Anderson becomes a younger George Willard, and Clyde, Ohio, becomes another Winesburg, Ohio--'a background on which to paint dreams of ... manhood'" (xi). Although the precise genesis for Tar is unknown, Anderson's inspiration apparently derived from interest in such a work by The Wom-

an's Home Companion. In early 1925, Anderson wrote to
his literary agent, Otto Liveright, that soon he would have
"something really good" to show the editorial board of Companion (xii). On April 18th of that year, the magazine paid
six thousand dollars for six installments of Tar. Tar: A
Midwest Childhood was first published in book form by Boni
and Liveright on 20 November 1926. White's excellent critical volume is the first edition printed since 1931.

(Further references: 375, 376, 377, 378, 380, 382, 423,
427, 435, 436, 437, 460, 466, 475, 476, 479, 482, 485,
495, 508, 509, 511, 518, 628, 631.)

The Triumph of the Egg

569.   Joseph, Gerhard. "The American Triumph of the
        Egg: Anderson's 'The Egg' and Fitzgerald's The
        Great Gatsby." Criticism, 7 (Spring 1965), pp. 131-
        40.
        Joseph suggests that both Anderson and Fitzgerald,
having been exposed to Freudian and Jungian commentary on
dream symbolism and archetypes, consciously and independ-
ently of each other utilized egg symbolism in their works to
expose the strengths and weaknesses of the American dream.
The egg as fact and symbol dominates the structure of Anderson's "The Egg," but does not possess such a radical
force in Fitzgerald's novel, The Great Gatsby. Joseph perceives a certain pessimistic irony which emerges in con-
sidering the two works side by side: "once a character attempts to mold his destiny, he is damned into an American
tragedy if he fails or if he succeeds" (140). And yet the
triumph of the egg is not complete. The attempt to man-
handle the egg of one's destiny embraces something worthy
and noble. The father in Anderson's story is dignified by
his humiliation, and likely the reader must agree with Nick
Carraway's final judgment of Gatsby: "you're worth the
whole bunch put together."

570.   Kingsbury, Stewart A. "A Structural Semantic
        Analysis of the 'Punch Line' of SA's Short Story,
        'The Egg.'" Papers from the Michigan Linguistic
        Society Meeting October 3, 1970. David Lawton, ed.
        Mt. Pleasant: Central Michigan University, 1971,
        p. 117.

571. Lovett, Robert Morss. "The Promise of SA. " Dial,
72 (January 1922), pp. 79-83.
Lovett interprets Anderson's work with "Apology
for Crudity" and Anderson's vision of American life--as it
is, without illusion--always at the back of his mind. With
a simplicity of style that penetrates to the very essence of
the American experience, Anderson creates in The Triumph
of the Egg a unified collection of stories that "give a single
reading of life, a sense of its immense burden, its pain, its
dreariness, its futile aspiration, its despair" (81-82). And
yet, in spite of the grim spectacle he paints, Anderson pre-
serves "the faith of the artist, the soul of the poet" (83).
Here lies in largest measure the promise of SA.

572. O'Brien, Edward Joseph. "SA and Waldo Frank. "
The Advance of the American Short Story. New York:
Dodd, Mead, 1923, pp. 247-65.
O'Brien sees Anderson spearheading the American
short story revolt against the mechanical techniques of O.
Henry, and that revolt symbolizes a personal and profound
revolution against a dull, societal conformity. O'Brien finds
in SA's short stories "studies in the sensitivity of a tired
people stirring with the first hurts of a newer and freer
life" (248). Waldo Frank's City Blocks strikes similar thematic notes and ranks just below Winesburg and The Triumph of the Egg.

573. West, Michael. "SA's Triumph: 'The Egg. ' "
American Quarterly, 20 (Winter 1968), pp. 675-93.
West undertakes his essay "in the conviction
that within the confines of a half-dozen or so stories, and
there only, Anderson is a truly memorable writer" (676).
"The Egg" numbers among the elite six. West dates the
composition of "The Egg" in the year 1918 (possibly early
summer), shortly after Anderson had completed writing
Winesburg. The story first appeared in the March, 1920,
issue of Dial as "The Triumph of the Egg. " In attempting
to underline the reasons for the story's brilliance, West
points to Anderson's prose style and appreciates the "facile,
vaguely evocative phrases of advertising" (680), the Biblical
phraseology, and the influence upon language and imagery
which derives from "Anderson's interest in contemporary
psychology" (682). In "The Egg" more than any other Anderson story, "language, images, details and themes coa-
lesce and enrich one another in extremely subtle relationships, the complexity of which verges on poetry and defies
logical exposition" (684). Central to Anderson's theme in

"The Egg" is getting people "to shake off the success dis-
ease. " West notes, "The success ethic has seldom taken a
harder beating than he [SA] administers in his description of
life on the proverbial chicken farm as it is actually lived"
(690).

"I Want to Know Why"

574. Brooks, Cleanth and Warren, Robert Penn. "I Want
      to Know Why. Interpretation. " Understanding Fiction.
      New York: Crofts, 1943, pp. 344-50.
      Brooks and Warren reprint the text of "I Want to
Know Why" and then offer an interpretation. They suggest
Anderson's tale is a story of initiation. The boy-narrator
learns something about the nature of evil: "he discovers
that good and bad are very intimately wedded to the very
nature of a man, and perhaps more important still, that it
is man's capacity for choice which makes good and evil
meaningful" (329). To the young boy the horse Sunstreak
embodies all that is most valuable and admirable in life:
he is beautiful, clean, courageous, honest. Jerry Tillford
and the "rotten-looking woman" at the "rummy farmhouse"
stand in vivid contrast to the qualities of the horse. The
scene of filth and ugliness disgusts and horrifies the boy--
he can hardly believe that Tillford would look upon the woman with the same gleam in his eyes he had had when view-
ing Sunstreak earlier in the afternoon. The boy comes to
understand that good and evil can be intimately allied in the
same man and that while a brute animal is always innocent,
a man can be either better or worse than a brute, depend-
ing upon the moral choices he makes.

575. Lawry, Jon. "Love and Betrayal in SA's 'I Want to
      Know Why. ' " Shenandoah, 13 (Spring 1962), pp. 46-
      54.
      Lawry analyzes the deceptively complex "I Want
to Know Why, " concluding that Anderson has asserted an element of hope in the boy's search for the secret of how to
"be a man ... and think straight and be O. K. " Lawry argues that if the boy "does pursue the answers--that love can
hopelessly move to its own betrayal, and that such a turn
may lie in his chosen path--he may in that knowledge be
'O. K. , ' for in such awareness must lie either the antidote
to betrayal, or, at the very worst, the ability to distinguish
love from self-indulgence, even if self-indulgence wins the
day" (54).

576.   Lesser, Simon O. "The Image of the Father: A
        Reading of 'My Kinsman, Major Molineux' and 'I Want
        to Know Why. '" Partisan Review, 22 (Summer 1955),
        pp. 372-90. (Reprinted in his Fiction and the Uncon-
        scious. Boston: Beacon 1957, pp. 224-34; and in
        Phillips, William. Art and Psychoanalysis. New
        York: Criterion Books, 1957, pp. 237-46.)
            Lesser offers a Freudian analysis of "I Want to
    Know Why" which emphasizes the boy-narrator's relation to
    Jerry Tillford. Lesser argues that the boy seeks an ideal-
    ized relationship with a man who is like his father but better
    than his father--a relationship devoid of sexuality. In Les-
    ser's interpretation, Anderson's tale "describes the frustra-
    tion of two dear but unfulfillable wishes of the adolescent
    boy. The first wish is to deny the sexuality of the parents
    in order to avoid competition with the father. . . . The sec-
    ond wish is for a love relationship with the father which,
    though idealized in some respects, is still so heavily cath-
    ected with libido that its satisfaction would involve both con-
    tinued dependence upon the father and a proprietary right to
    his affection" (389-90). Lesser's argument attempts to ex-
    plain the impact of the story as it is perceived by the un-
    conscious intellect.

577.   Parish, John E. "The Silent Father in Anderson's
        'I Want to Know Why. '" Rice University Studies, 51
        (Winter 1965), pp. 49-57.
            Parish argues that Andersonian critics have
    either ignored or seriously misjudged the father of the boy-
    narrator in "I Want to Know Why." Parish interprets the
    lawyer-father as an understanding man "who loves his son
    deeply, observes him constantly--from a distance--and wise-
    ly says to his wife: 'Let him alone'" (50). Positively old-
    fashioned, he deserves the reader's respect and admiration.
    The young narrator's moral development begins beneath the
    example of a wise parent.

(Further references: 375, 376, 377, 379, 380, 382, 423,
433, 434, 435, 460, 463, 464, 472, 475, 509, 510, 513,
518, 628.)

                    Windy McPherson's Son

578.   Dell, Floyd. "On Being SA's Literary Father."
        Newberry Library Bulletin, 5 (December 1961), pp.

315-21.

Dell recalls his efforts--ultimately successful--
to secure a publisher for Anderson's first novel. On his
role as literary parent, Dell notes: "This business of being
a literary father is something that I was never cut out for,
and I am sure that I managed it badly" (320). He happily re-
linquished his role to a second literary father, Paul Rosenfeld.

579.   Frank, Waldo. "Emerging Greatness. " The Seven
        Arts, 1 (November 1916), pp. 73-78. (Reprinted in
        Frank's Salvos, An Informal Book About Books and
        Plays. New York: Boni and Liveright, 1924, pp. 31-
        40; and in The Achievement of SA. Ray Lewis White,
        ed. Chapel Hill: University of North Carolina Press,
        1966, pp. 20-24.)
        Frank's analysis of Windy McPherson's Son recog-
nizes the unsatisfactory conclusion of the novel, but also
recognizes the creative potential of its author and predicts a
continuing artistic growth.

580.   Hackett, Francis. "A New Novelist. " Horizons.
        New York: Huebsch, 1918, pp. 50-56.
        In Horizons Francis Hackett gathers together re-
views written over a period of ten years for The Chicago
Evening Post and The New Republic. Although the critic
finds Windy flawed by lengthy expression of those "thoughts
which so enamor the young novelist" and "so often break in
the weaving like a gossamer too thin to be spun" (51),
Hackett appreciates the flood of midwestern humanity that
people the book. In Windy McPherson's Son, Anderson "has
made the America of the small town his own, its stridencies
and heart-hungers and thin spiral fires" (55).

581.   Morris, Wright. "Introduction. " Windy McPherson's
        Son. Chicago: University of Chicago Press, 1965,
        pp. vii-xix.
        Windy McPherson's Son was Anderson's first pub-
lished novel, but Morris cautions: "To think of it as a first
novel is more distracting than helpful" (ix). The reader
should bear in mind Anderson's maturity (he was forty years
old at the time), his writing experience, and the fact that his
writing never proved to be at its best in the novel form.
Nonetheless, most 'writers of substance give us something
of their measure, and their enduring preoccupations, in the
first book they publish, and McPherson is no exception. The
reader of Anderson will find both the past and the future in

it. It reveals what he had learned of writing from books, and what he believed he had learned from living" (ix-x). Morris suggests that Sam McPherson anticipates the grotesques of Winesburg and that McPherson is furthermore a full-length portrait of Anderson himself. Morris also comments upon the impact of Chicago on the writer's imagination. Chicago encompassed the parameters of life and death and clearly influenced Anderson's writing. To the midwest American, "Chicago was money. Chicago was fame. Chicago was the freedom to live as one pleased. It was also death to the soul" (xiii). Anderson captures the essence of the Chicago experience.

(Further references: 375, 376, 377, 378, 380, 382, 391, 405, 423, 424, 427, 433, 434, 435, 438, 444, 446, 448, 453, 456, 457, 460, 463, 466, 471, 472, 479, 482, 483, 485, 491, 495, 498, 508, 509, 510, 511, 516, 518, 596, 631.)

Winesburg, Ohio

582.   Abcarian, Richard. "Innocence and Experience in Winesburg." University Review, 35 (Winter 1968), pp. 95-105.
        Abcarian cautions against those interpretations of Winesburg which tend to overemphasize the role of George Willard forcing Anderson's work to read like "a kind of parable of the artist in the modern world" (95). He focuses attention upon a recurring pattern of frustration and wasted human potential. This pattern governs the narrative structure of at least twelve of Winesburg's twenty-one tales and frequently involves the grotesques in futile attempts to recover the lost innocence of their youths. In only one story, "Sophistication," does Anderson assert an element of hope: George Willard and Helen White achieve a moment of total communication and understanding. Unlike the grotesques they embody youthful innocence, "a state of grace making their communion possible" (102).

583.   Allen, Walter. The Urgent West: The American Dream and Modern Man. New York: Dutton, 1969, pp. 195-97, 200.
        Allen assesses Anderson's place in the history of American letters: "Though there had been great American short story writers--Hawthorne, Poe, James--before Ander-

son, he stands out as the founding father of the modern short
story in America" (196). Allen briefly comments on what he
considers the best of SA's work, Winesburg, and notes that
it deals with the lives of men and women "who have discovered they are isolated and unique" (196).

584.   Anderson, David D. "SA's Moment of Insights."
       Critical Studies in American Literature: A Collection
       of Essays. Karachi, Pakistan: University of Karachi,
       1964, pp. 108-31.
            In a brilliantly written, highly perceptive essay
David D. Anderson analyzes Winesburg in terms of "moments
of insight" that enables SA to peer beneath the surface of reality and glean the essence of individual human experience.
In Winesburg, SA "attained artistic insight in a form eminently suited to his own peculiar talents for attaining empathy with other human beings" (110). The tales of Winesburg explore the problems of individual isolation, and SA
approaches these problems in their "simplest individual
terms, seeking understanding through intuitive perception of
the essence of individuality" (113). To a certain degree,
Winesburg may also be seen as a novel of initiation or a
portrait of the artist as a young man, but David Anderson
asserts, "The book's chief merit is that it is about people.
Willard's role is secondary to the people about whom each
individual story centers.... For the first time Anderson
was attempting to write fiction rather than disguised autobiography, and the breadth of individuality in the stories
shows the success of the attempt" (123).

585.   Baker, Carlos. "SA's Winesburg: A Reprise."
       Virginia Quarterly Review, 48 (Autumn 1972, pp.
       568-79.
            Baker utilizes many of Anderson's own public ut-
terances to provide the proper historical framework for his
essay on Winesburg. He documents Anderson's concern for
several underlying themes: human sexuality, escape and pursuit, self-sacrificial love, materialism, American religiosity,
and suggests four key terms for coming to grips with recur-
rent thematic patterns in the book: deprivation, search, release, and repression (575). He sees George Willard as the
"chief agent of unification both for the book itself and for the
brooding residents of Winesburg" (578) and concludes that
Anderson's book is a kind of "informal 'Bildungsroman' with
George as the hero" (578).

586.   Bennett, Josiah Q. "Winesburg Revisited." The

Serif, 7 (September 1970), pp. 80-82.
Mr. Bennett's concise bibliographic note corrob-
orates certain textual assessments made by William L.
Phillips in his 1951 article, "The First Printing of SA's
Winesburg, Ohio," and articulates certain technical findings
regarding the first impression of Winesburg.

587. Berland, Alwyn. "SA and the Pathetic Grotesque."
      Western Review, 15 (Winter 1951), pp. 135-58.
      Berland analyzes Winesburg in terms of a per-
vasive sense of pathos that finds its most elaborate articula-
tion in the opening story, "The Book of the Grotesque."
There Anderson tells us that "the moment one of the people
took one of the truths to himself, called it his truth, and
tried to live his life by it, he became a grotesque and the
truth he embraced became a falsehood." In the world of
Winesburg, all characters--including the old artist figure
in "The Book of the Grotesque"--become twisted by the
truths they embrace: "No one escapes. There are no al-
ternatives; even death is pathetic because it reveals what
ideal life might be if it were more than a dream" (138).

588. Bort, Barr D. "Winesburg, Ohio: The Escape from
      Isolation." Midwest Quarterly, 11 (Summer 1970),
      pp. 443-56.
      Bort argues that Andersonian criticism has recog-
nized the general theme of isolation and loneliness and the
desperate need for meaningful communication. But what has
not been fully understood about Winesburg is that the con-
tinual frustration of characters seeking communication provides a "context out of which arise a few luminous moments
of understanding. Precious anticipated communion is the
real theme of the book" (452). Some characters seek communion in sex, but are inevitably disillusioned. Only a few--
Dr. Reefy and George Willard in particular--achieve moments of complete understanding. It is these few and evanescent moments that make life livable, moments when human community is realized, "even if that community be only
two" (456).

589. Bowden, Edwin T. The Dungeon of the Heart: Hu-
      man Isolation and the American Novel. New York:
      Macmillan, 1961, pp. 114-24.
      Within the context of The Dungeon of the Heart,
Edwin T. Bowden analyzes the problem of human isolation
as a recurring theme in the development of the American
novel. His examination of Winesburg offers a proper his-

torical perspective of the isolation theme and places Anderson squarely within a tradition that includes Nathaniel Hawthorne, Mark Twain, W. D. Howells, Henry James, and other giants of American letters. Bowden sees Winesburg as a "collection of interrelated sketches of isolated and lonely people in a small commonplace Ohio town" (114) and contends that Anderson's treatment of the problem of isolation is much more intense than most of his predecessors would have allowed.

590.   Browning, Chris. "Kate Swift: SA's Creative Eros."
       Tennessee Studies in Literature, 13 (1968), pp. 141-
       48.
       Ms. Browning sees Anderson's portrait of the teacher, Kate Swift, as an embodiment of his ideal woman, endowed with "intelligence, education, energy and passion for life, independence of spirit" (141). Further, she is the avatar of "continuity of life, in both the creative and spiritual realms" (141). Borrowing a term from Ludwig Lewisohn, Browning describes Kate Swift as Anderson's "creative Eros," a female embodiment of spiritual and biological strength. Particularly for George Willard and the Reverend Curtis Hartman, she becomes an essential symbol of creativity.

591.   Bucco, Martin. "A Reading of SA's 'Hands.'"
       Colorado State Review, 1 (Spring 1966), pp. 5-8.
       A concise, insightful analysis of "Hands," Bucco's essay discusses narrative technique, structure, setting, dark humor, and theme in Anderson's story. Always struggling against the terrifying saloon keeper's command to "Keep your hands to yourself," Biddlebaum stands a lonely, pathetic figure, who nonetheless can urge George Willard to dream, to idealize, to seek life's essences.

592.   Budd, Louis J. "The Grotesques of Anderson and
       Wolfe." Modern Fiction Studies, 5 (Winter 1959-60),
       pp. 304-10.
       Budd suggests that Wolfe's familiarity with Winesburg, Ohio "contributed to the viewpoint, structure, and even the rhetoric of Look Homeward" (309). He points to specific similarities between the two books: 1) "life's frightening meaninglessness" balances against "a tender belief in life's magic" (306); 2) vision of man's isolation and loneliness; 3) the adolescent struggle toward discovery in both George Willard and Eugene Gant; 4) the very loose structure and autobiographical technique; and 5) "'Sophistication' foreshadows in detail Look Homeward's closing scene" (308).

593. Ciancio, Ralph. " 'The Sweetness of the Twisted Apples:' Unity of Vision in Winesburg, Ohio. " PMLA, 87 (October 1972), pp. 994-1006.

Ciancio recognizes the critical controversy that rages over the relation of the first of the Winesburg tales, "The Book of the Grotesques," to the whole of Anderson's work, and argues that an understanding of the prologue story is important to a consideration of Winesburg's thematic implications and philosophical unity. He points out the simple, but seldom-stated notion that Anderson's attitude varies toward his grotesques: some are horrible, some amusing, some even beautiful. But in their grotesqueness, they attain something of the "sweetness of the twisted apples. " Their essence is gathered into gnarls of dreams--frequently beautiful dreams--and fanatacism. But in their grotesqueness they avoid, at least, the banality of the clods who dominate the official life of the town (996). In his growth toward maturity and the vocational calling of the artist, George Willard can learn from the grotesques--learn about dreams and the life of the imagination and escape finally from the "debilitating provincialism of Winesburg" (996).

594. Cowley, Malcolm. "Anderson's Lost Days of Innocence. " New Republic, 142 (15 February 1960), pp. 16-18.

Cowley's short, perceptive article underlines Anderson's influence upon the generation of writers that followed him in American letters. The list of indebtedness is impressive: Hemingway, Faulkner, Wolfe, Steinbeck, Caldwell, Saroyan, Henry Miller. What Anderson did for these writers "was to open vistas by finding new depths or breadths of feeling in everyday American life" (16). In Anderson's own work, these insights became epiphanies, moments when the essential reality of a character stands naked, stripped of its worldly veils. These moments were, in general, moments without sequel, which explains why none of Anderson's novels succeeded as unified works. Only in Winesburg was Anderson fully successful. Cowley suggests these reasons: "because it was conceived as a whole, because Anderson had found a subject that released his buried emotions, and because most of it was written in the same burst of inspiration, so that it gathered force as it went along" (17).

595. Cowley, Malcolm. "Introduction. " Winesburg, Ohio. 1919; reprint, New York: Viking Press, 1960, pp. 1-15.

Cowley offers an appropriately semi-biographical

introduction to Anderson and his major work while asserting
that Anderson was a story teller and that his art "was of a
special type, belonging to an oral rather than a written tradition" (5). Anderson, he argues, is at his best in painting
miniatures of fiction and creating moments of aliveness--
epiphanies--when characters crash through the walls of isolation to find evanescent moments of meaningful communication. Anderson "had that gift for summing up, for pouring
a lifetime into a moment" (8). Winesburg embraces the
best of Anderson; it "is a work of love, an attempt to break
down the walls that divide one person from another, and also, in its own fashion, a celebration of small-town life in
the last days of good will and innocence" (15).

596.   Ferres, John H.   "The Nostalgia of Winesburg,
        Ohio." Newberry Library Bulletin, 6 (July 1971),
        pp. 235-42.
        Ferres posits the interesting argument that
Winesburg continues to appeal to contemporary readers not
so much because of its carefully repeated theme of loneliness and isolation nor because of its revolt-from-the-village
statement, but because of a powerful and pervasive nostalgia
that recalls a "pre-industrial, pre-Civil War mid-America"
(237). Especially in the seventies, as man contemplates an
environment of polluted air and waterways, drastic food
shortages and starving children, and the omnipresent threat
of nuclear holocaust, the simple agrarian life of Winesburg
seems almost utopian.

597.   Ferres, John H.   "Winesburg, Ohio at Fifty." Hof-
        stra Review, 4 (Autumn 1969), pp. 5-10.

598.   Frank, Waldo.   "Winesburg, Ohio after Twenty
        Years." Story, 19 (September-October 1941), pp. 29-
        33.
        Though now somewhat dated, Mr. Frank's as-
sessment of Anderson's narrative technique in Winesburg
remains important to any serious study of narrative structure. In most of the tales, "the Winesburg design is quite
uniform: a theme statement of a character with his mood,
followed by a recounting of actions that are merely variations on the theme. These variations make incarnate what
has already been revealed to the reader" (29).

599.   Fussell, Edwin.   "Winesburg, Ohio: Art and Isola-
        lation." Modern Fiction Studies, 6 (Summer 1960),
        pp. 106-115.

Fussell places Winesburg within the tradition of the Bildungsroman, though it is not merely a "portrait of the artist as a young man." He accords Winesburg high praise: "there are few works of modern fiction in which the artist's relations with ordinary men are seen with such a happy blend of acuity and clarity, few works of any age in which the artist and ordinary men are seen so well as fitting together in a complementary union that permits us to make distinctions of relative value while at the same time retaining a universally different sense of equal dignity" (108-09). George Willard serves the grotesques as an instrument for expressing their pent-up truths, but perhaps even more significantly, the grotesques have much to give to Willard. The relation of the artist to the grotesques is vital to an understanding of the steadily maturing progression that leads to Willard's "Departure." Willard learns the high truth of human isolation, but unlike the grotesques he is able to live with it. "His willingness to do so is at once the sign of his maturity and the pledge of his incipient artistic ability" (111).

600.   Gochberg, Donald. "Stagnation and Growth: The Emergence of George Willard." Expression, 4 (Winter 1960), pp. 29-35.

601.   Gold, Herbert. "The Purity and Cunning of SA." Hudson Review, 10 (Winter 1957-58), pp. 548-59. (Note: reprinted in Shapiro, Charles, ed. Twelve Original Essays on Great American Novels. Detroit: Wayne State University Press, 1958, pp. 196-209.)

Gold analyzes Winesburg largely in terms of the intense personal relationship that existed between Anderson and his work: all of Anderson's work, "the abysmal failures and the successes which have helped to construct the vision Americans have of themselves, represents an innocent, factitious, improvised, schemed reflection and elaboration of the elements of his own life" (550). He particularly emphasizes the epiphany-like quality found in Anderson's best tales--a quality that enables Anderson to capture the essence of love, hope, failed ambition, weakness, and loneliness.

602.   Hilfer, Anthony C. "Masters and Anderson." The Revolt from the Village. Chapel Hill: University of North Carolina Press, 1969, pp. 137-57.

Hilfer argues that Winesburg may be read as a series of closely interrelated stories dealing with the problems of human loneliness and isolation, and that America's Coming of Age by Van Wyck Brooks may be a useful critical

tool in studying the "values and insights that lie beneath
Winesburg" (157). The dominant emotion in Anderson's
masterpiece is pathos. Characters engage in pathetic attempts to "reach out, to break through the walls of emotional repression, to express their inner voices to another
human being" (152). Winesburg was, no doubt, influenced
by Masters' Spoon River Anthology, but "the major difference
between the books is that while Masters' characters hide
their feelings, Anderson's inarticulate characters hardly
know what their feelings are" (148).

603.   Howe, Irving. "SA, Winesburg, Ohio. " The Ameri-
        can Novel from James Fenimore Cooper to William
        Faulkner. Wallace Stegner, ed. New York: Basic
        Books, 1965, pp. 154-65.

604.   Ingram, Forrest L. "SA: Winesburg, Ohio. " Repre-
        sentative Short Story Cycles of the Twentieth Century:
        Studies in a Literary Genre. The Hague: Mouton,
        1971, pp. 143-99.
            Ingram argues at length that the unity of Wines-
        burg is that of a short story cycle, both in the sense of a
        connected series and in the sense of a recurring develop-
        ment in a set of narratives. According to Ingram, the "ac-
        tion of the book consists in the gradual emergence, from
        conception in 'The Book of the Grotesque,' to maturity in
        'Departure,' of a fictive community in the distortive memory
        of the book's single narrator; and of a return, in 'Depar-
        ture,' to the initial (now modified) situation--which had been
        presented in 'The Book of the Grotesque'" (147).

605.   Joselyn, Sister M. , O. S. B. "SA and the Lyric
        Story. " The Twenties: Poetry and Prose. Richard
        E. Langford and William E. Taylor, eds. Deland,
        Florida: Everett Edwards Press, 1966, pp. 70-73.
            Sister Joselyn suggests that perhaps the "sanest"
        way to view Winesburg is as an "uneven collection, ... a
        special kind of amalgam of naturalism and lyricism" (70).
        She notes that Anderson's best stories always climax in
        epiphany-like moments and that from these moments the
        reader "derives an unmistakable sense of authentic experi-
        ence being worked out from within in the manner of the
        great Russians--Turgenev and Chekhov--with their unparal-
        leled suggestiveness and extreme economy of means" (72).

606.   Kramer, Dale. Chicago Renaissance: The Literary
        Life in the Midwest, 1900-1930. New York: Apple-

ton-Century, 1966, pp. 37-51, 288-305.
Kramer devotes two full chapters to Anderson in his scholarly, fascinating examination of the Chicago Renaissance. The first offers a concise biography; the second, penetrating insights into Anderson's earliest works, focusing primarily upon Winesburg. Along with William Phillips' article (no. 619), Kramer's essay provides excellent background on the writing and assembling of the stories that comprise Winesburg, Ohio.

607.   Laughlin, Rosemary M.   " 'Godliness' and the American Dream in Winesburg, Ohio. "   Twentieth Century Literature, 13 (July 1967), pp. 97-103.
Laughlin argues for the consonance of "Godliness" within the symbolic and thematic structure of Winesburg, Ohio, thus offering a positive evaluation of the largest of Winesburg's tales in relation to the whole of Anderson's book.

608.   Lorch, Thomas M.   "The Choreographic Structure of Winesburg, Ohio. "   College Language Association Journal, 12 (September 1968), pp. 56-65.
Lorch argues for greater structural unity than most critics would allow. He finds the metaphor from the dance particularly appropriate for structurally assessing a book that emphasizes symbol rather than action or even "highly developed characters" (57). Lorch suggests, the "dance exhibits that combination of formally patterned spatial relationships and temporal development which most closely resembles the structure of Winesburg, Ohio" (56). Ultimately, he finds that common patterns of action and character and the recurring motif of the search for self-realization and fulfillment constitute a structure that unite Winesburg into "a unique organic work of art" (65).

609.   Love, Glen A.   "Winesburg, Ohio and the Rhetoric of Silence. "   American Literature, 40 (March 1968), pp. 38-57.
Love argues that Anderson's "concern about the isolation of man from nature and from his fellow man, his aversion to noise--and especially the noise of words and talk--are set in uneasy balance against his preoccupation with, and reverence for, the psychic states associated with the natural world, with pastoral life, and with silence as a measure of inner significance" (38). Within Winesburg the tranquility and purity of pastoral settings contrast with the noise and jangle and filth of the industrialized town. Significantly, Wing Biddlebaum's Utopian dream of perfect human

communication is set in a "pastoral golden age." Love emphasizes the importance of George Willard, who serves the
grotesques as an instrument of verbal release and who realizes his own moment of perfect communication with Helen
White--a communication that is utterly non-verbal. In contrast to the spiritual atrophy of the grotesques, Willard
grows and matures into a young artist who bids silent fare-
well to Winesburg, but who carried with him the sacred
doubt that "words can communicate anything but our final
isolation from one another" (57).

610.   Luedtke, Luther S. "SA, Thomas Hardy and 'Tandy.'"
        Modern Fiction Studies, 20 (Winter 1974-75), pp.
        531-39.
            Luedtke perceives similar powerful themes run-
ning through the works of Anderson and Hardy. Both "stud-
ied the fragmentation and spiritual hunger of rural backwaters
left by the sweep of modern technology and commerce, and
both created mythic communities ... in which to examine the
condition of man, woman, and the earth in the new age" (531).
He suggests that "Tandy" of Winesburg, Ohio evidences Anderson's strongest indebtedness to Hardy. In Anderson's
characterization of the stranger, Tom Hard, and Hard's
daughter, he creates a "curious vignette of Jude Fawley"
(533). Parallels between the stranger and Jude "exist in
both their objects of longing and their causes of despair"
(533). Jude, like the stranger, desperately "wanted something to love." Further, the tender vision of Tandy--"strong
to be loved"--"reminds us of the perfected beauty of Sue's
body and spirit" (534). The story "Tandy" stands nearly an
isolated manifesto in Winesburg proclaiming a faith that modern man and woman may "still make an uncertain way back
to a natural relation with one another and the world in which
they live" (540).

611.   McCleer, John H. "Christ Symbolism in Winesburg,
        Ohio." Discourse, 4 (Summer 1961), pp. 168-81.
            McCleer perceives a pattern of Christ symbolism
recurring throughout Winesburg and perhaps best symbolized
by the grotesque Dr. Parcival who warns George Willard,
"Everyone in the whole world is Christ and they are all
crucified." Willard seems to quest after a "latter-day Holy
Grail, a cup of explanation in which to catch man's spilled
blood and endow it with significance, a way of accounting for
man's suffering" (171). Willard's ultimate departure from
Winesburg "restates the central argument of the book: only
when man gives precedence to his spirit over material things
will he wear his sufferings lightly" (179).

612.   McDonald, W. R.   "Winesburg, Ohio: Tales of Isola-
       tion. " University Review, 35 (Spring 1969), pp. 237-
       40.
            McDonald finds within Winesburg a recurrent pat-
tern of isolated individuals, each "yearning to escape his own
isolation" (237) and searching for an "understanding companion" (237) who can help to facilitate a meaningful moment
of communication. Many of the characters in Winesburg are
emotional cripples, unable for the most part to escape their
utter loneliness. A few, however (most importantly, George
Willard in "Sophistication"), achieve those rare moments of
love and understanding that make the "mature lives of men
and women in the modern world possible. "

613.   Mahoney, John J.   "An Analysis of Winesburg, Ohio. "
       Journal of Aesthetics and Art Criticism, 15 (Decem-
       ber 1956), pp. 245-52.
            In attempting to determine the genesis of aesthetic
effect in Winesburg, Mahoney employs a method based upon
the terms, voice and address. His detailed analysis results
in the conclusion that Winesburg owes much of its peculiar
emotional effect to the "device of the impassioned soliloquy"
(252).

614.   Maresca, Carol J.   "Gestures as Meaning in SA's
       Winesburg, Ohio. " College Language Association
       Journal, 9 (March 1966), pp. 279-83.
            Ms. Maresca argues that dialogue is conspicu-
ously limited in Winesburg and that Anderson chooses to em-
phasize characters' exterior being, actions, and appearances.
As Kate Swift tells George Willard, one must learn "to know
what people are thinking about, not what they say. " Maresca
finds that conversation, for Anderson, is "at best, an ele-
mentary and often a false indication of a man's personality"
(279). She discusses in some detail Winesburg's hand and
eye imagery and its relation to theme and meaning.

615.   Mellard, James M.   "Narrative Forms in Winesburg,
       Ohio. " PMLA, 83 (October 1968), pp. 1304-12.
            Mellard disagrees with those critics who would
argue for one narrative form in Winesburg. Rather, he suggests four distinct narrative forms: those "1) that focus on
a central symbol, " e. g. , "The Book of the Grotesque, "
"Hands"; 2) that portray a character type, e. g. , "Mother, "
"A Man of Ideas"; 3) that delineate a quality, state, or
"truth, " e. g. , "Loneliness, " "Death"; and 4) "that depict a
simple plot development, " e. g. , "Adventure, " "The Untold
Lie" (1304). He labels these narrative types "symbolic, em-

blematic ... thematic ... and stories of incident" (1304),
respectively.

616. Murphy, G. D. "The Theme of Sublimation in An-
      derson's Winesburg, Ohio. " Modern Fiction Studies,
      13 (Summer 1967), pp. 237-46.
      Murphy argues that Anderson displays a markedly
cautious attitude toward sex in Winesburg, and that this attitude exerts a powerful influence upon the form and theme
of the book. Murphy classifies Winesburg's grotesques into
four types based upon their responses to sexual emotion:
1) those repelled by sexual feelings and who seek to avoid
the fact of sex; 2) those who complacently accept sex and
see nothing beyond it; 3) those who settle for sex while wistfully perceiving there is something that transcends it; and
4) those few who "perceive the role of sexuality in Anderson's own terms and experience it as a prelude--a material
reflection of a kind of Platonic perfection of the soul" (238).

617. Pawlowski, Robert S. "The Process of Observation:
      Winesburg, Ohio and The Golden Apples. " University
      Review, 37 (Summer 1971), pp. 292-98.
      Pawlowski analyzes artistic similarities between
Anderson's Winesburg, Ohio and Eudora Welty's The Golden
Apples: both volumes are collections of short stories in
which a set of characters appear and reappear; both employ
a setting--the small town--common to all the stories. In
each work, characters are "condemned to solitariness" (293)
and because of "the inability to communicate and to act,
neither book has a hero" (293). George Willard and King
MacLain are no doubt main figures, but "each plays a greater role as motif than as hero" (293). The authors, Pawlowski argues, may be likened to cubistic painters: "The
events in the collection are, as are the events on the cubist's
canvas, so loosely connected that the viewer is at a loss to
learn at once their specific relationship to each other and
to the design as a whole. There is no plot in either collection; yet the events have a sequential order and an organic
identity" (296).

618. Phillips, William L. "The First Printing of SA's
      Winesburg, Ohio. " Studies in Bibliography, 4 (1951-
      52), pp. 211-13.
      Phillips cites a 1919 New York Sun review of
Winesburg that rails at Anderson's bad grammar in a sentence found on page 86, line 5. The first printing sentence
reads: "an intense silence seemed to lay over everything. "

According to Phillips' research, all editions after the first
edition correct the grammatical error. From the second
edition on, the word "lie" replaces "lay." Thus, first print-
ings can be identified by the "lay" reading.

619.   Phillips, William L. "How SA Wrote Winesburg,
        Ohio." American Literature, 23 (March 1951), pp.
        7-30.
        Basing his judgments upon exhaustive examination
of the Winesburg manuscripts at the Newberry Library,
Phillips asserts that "the book was conceived as a unit, knit
together, however loosely, by the idea of the first tale, 'The
Book of the Grotesque,' and consisting of individual sketches
which derived additional power from each other, not, as
anthologists of Anderson repeatedly suggest, a collection of
short stories which can be separated from each other without
loss of effect" (7). Examination of the manuscript further
suggests that Anderson's own accounts of his writing were
"subjective and romanticized" (9), though the stories were
apparently written over a relatively short period of time
(1915-1916), one leading readily to another. Phillips' article
remains one of the most significant in the entire canon of
Winesburg criticism, for he offers persuasive evidence regarding both Anderson's creative method and the order and
manner in which the stories that comprise Winesburg were
written.

620.   Picht, Douglas R. "Anderson's Use of Tactile Im-
        agery in Winesburg, Ohio." Research Studies of
        Washington State University, 35 (June 1967), pp. 176-
        78.

621.   Rideout, Walter B. "The Simplicity of Winesburg,
        Ohio." Shenandoah, 13 (Spring 1962), pp. 20-31.
        In this highly readable essay, Rideout suggests
that the simplicity of language and form so apparent in a
first reading of Winesburg becomes upon second or subse-
quent readings a paradoxically complex simplicity: "What
had once seemed to have the clarity of water held in the
hand begins to take on instead its elusiveness" (20). In
order to come to grips with Winesburg, one must peer beneath the surface of the characters' lives "to perceive the
intricate mesh of impulses, desires, drives growing down
in the dark, unrevealed parts of the personality" (23).
George Willard, the young artist figure, gradually learns to
see beneath the apparent reality of things to the true reality
below. His progression in Winesburg from innocence to ex-

perience, from ignorance to understanding, is vitally and in-
separably tied to his "growing desire to be a creative writer
and his increasing awareness of the meaning of that vocation" (27).

622.   Rideout, Walter B.   " 'The Tale of Perfect Balance':
        SA's 'The Untold Lie.' " Newberry Library Bulletin,
        6 (July 1971), pp. 243-50.
        In A Story Teller's Story Anderson indicates his
primary goal as a writer of short fiction: to create "the
tale of perfect balance, all the elements of the tale understood, an infinite number of minute adjustments perfectly
made, the power of self-criticism fully at work. ... " Rideout convincingly argues that "The Untold Lie" achieves Anderson's goal, creating in a carefully conceived and executed
pattern of opposites, "an art that paradoxically conceals art"
(250).

623.   Rogers, Douglas G.   "Development of the Artist in
        Winesburg, Ohio. " Studies in the Twentieth Century,
        10 (Fall 1972), pp. 91-99.
        Rogers asserts that Winesburg is the cumulative
story of "walls"--"people walled-in, struggling to communicate, desperately attempting to reach out and touch those
around them, yet for the most part unable to crash the walls,
unable to communicate meaningfully, unable to escape their
utter isolation" (91).   George Willard, the young artist figure, serves as an instrument through which the grotesques
tell their stories, a means of expressing the truths they
live by, a way of transcending the walls which envelop them.
Most of the grotesques remain isolated within the walls of
self, but in "Sophistication" Willard transcends those walls
and realizes a moment of genuine communication.   His experiences in Winesburg have enabled him to understand what
makes life bearable, livable, beautiful.   His final "Departure" signifies the maturity of his attitude as an artist.
There is the hope that Willard will somehow combine the
realities of his Winesburg years with the dreams, the imagination, of manhood.

624.   San Juan, Epifanio, Jr.   "Vision and Reality: A Re-
        consideration of SA's Winesburg, Ohio. " American
        Literature, 35 (May 1963), pp. 137-55.
        Arguing against the generally negative consensus
of critical opinion about Anderson's protagonists, San Juan
asserts that characters like Dr. Parcival incarnate "the in-
tensest energy and amplitude of imagination which Anderson

prized above all other qualities" (139). Parcival and certain
other Winesburg protagonists testify to the triumph of possi-
bility and free initiative and stand in vivid contrast against
the doctrine-bound moralizing of the Tom Willards of the
town. San Juan finds Anderson figures persuasively "round."
Anderson achieves this roundness by getting below the surface
to capture a character's inner struggles. Frequently he
touches upon empiric truth, embodying "abstractions in some
organic or physical act, thereby capturing just the exact
rhythm and movement of body and speech on which drama in
fiction depends" (142). San Juan's discerning analysis of
Winesburg examines Anderson's method of characterization,
patterns of imagery, prose rhythm, and use of irony. He
concludes with Faulkner that Anderson exemplifies the artist
"to whom nothing is lost."

625. Stegner, Wallace, and others. The Writer's Art.
     Boston: Heath, 1950, pp. 152-45.
     The editors reprint "Adventure" from Winesburg
and proceed to a brief analysis that focuses upon the theme
of loneliness and isolation. Presentation of the isolation
theme serves also to reinforce a belief in "the very positive
condition of human companionship, love, human dependence"
(145).

626. Stouck, David. "Winesburg, Ohio and the Failure of
     Art." Twentieth Century Literature, 15 (October
     1969), pp. 145-51.
     Stouck's interpretation encompasses the view that
Winesburg may be seen as "recording an artist's growth toward maturity" (146). He calls Elizabeth Willard's prayer
that "this my boy be allowed to express something for us
both." His essay then concerns the extent to which the
prayer is fulfilled. "Or to put it in another way, to what
degree can art fulfill those human needs left unsatisfied by
life?" (147). Stouck's answers to his self-imposed question
run counter to the bulk of Andersonian criticism. He perceives just below the surface in the narrative voice of
Winesburg a "desperate sense of futility" (150) and finds
the book's central focus lies in a recurring motif of "loneliness and the failure of self-realization" (150). Stouck
posits the interesting notion that the "sophisticated narrator"
(151) of Winesburg is an older George Willard who creates
a book that "might be described as a series of tombstones
erected out of love for the people he once knew" (151).
Finally, the artist cannot "save his people," and Stouck concludes that "art can bring awareness, but cannot substitute
for life" (151).

627.   Sullivan, John H.   "Winesburg Revisited."   Antioch
        Review, 20 (Summer 1960), pp. 213-21.
                 Sullivan's interesting and unusual article offers
no critical treatment of Winesburg, but instead a folksy
rambling through Clyde, Ohio, the physical prototype for
Anderson's mythic town.   Clyde of the 1950's is much different from the town of Anderson's boyhood: industry has
significantly increased while the railroad is no longer so
active.   Yet the town retains certain pastoral qualities, and
the population has increased only slightly.   Strangely enough,
Clyde, Ohio--unlike Camden, Anderson's birthplace--does not
cherish the memory of Sherwood Anderson.   Indeed, Sullivan
predicts that "Anderson may someday be remembered in
American literature as the townsman from Clyde, but in
Clyde he is almost sure to be forgotten" (221).

628.   Tanner, Tony.   "SA's Little Things."   The Reign
        of Wonder: Naivety and Reality in American Litera-
        ture.   Cambridge: Cambridge University Press,
        1965, pp. 205-227.
                 Tanner places special emphasis upon Anderson's
own remarks in "Apology for Crudity," where SA attempted
to clarify his thoughts on American writing.   There, Anderson clearly calls for a "crude and childlike" prose which as
Tanner points out, "succumbs to the facts ... not a probe
which takes issue with them or disdains them" (205).   Tanner interprets Anderson as the type of artist who has great
"capacity for sensory response, willingly capitulating to the
environment to let it feel through him" (207).   Pointing to
Winesburg as SA's most significant work, Tanner indicates
the particular qualities he finds in Anderson's prose: 1) the
inclusion of seemingly gratuitous details; 2) the sudden
thrusting of facts before the reader without prior introduction; 3) the head-on confronting of facts that "has the effect
of neutralizing experience: life's intensities come to us
muted" (209); 4) creation of epiphanies--powerful concentration that captures the essence of moments; 5) simple basic
sentence structure, efficiently transmitting information about
material action; 6) profound subjective identification with the
world of his fiction; 7) an ability to move from concretely
delineated detail to vague mystical generalization.   Ultimately, in Tanner's view, the "shortcomings of Anderson's writing are a function of his chosen strategy: he sees some
things freshly, clearly, honestly. But he sees only 'little
things' ... Ironically enough it is finally his writing which
undervalues the people and places he writes about" (217),
even though he writes with empathy and compassion.

629. Thurston, Jarvis A. "Anderson and Winesburg:
Mysticism and Craft." Accent, 16 (Spring 1956), pp.
107-28.
Thurston argues that critics have generally paid
too little attention to Anderson's mysticism, which as an
idea expressible outside of art "goes little beyond a rejection
of materialism and a yearning for the selflessness of permanent 'brotherhood'" (107). Anderson's mystic religiosity seriously influences his view of the nature and function of art and
directly affects such problems of craft as "characterization,
action, setting, point of view, style, and structure" (107).
In Winesburg, Anderson strikes out at the industrialism of
contemporary America which "is depersonalizing mankind
and destroying the spiritual entity that is the source of all
beauty in human relations and art" (111). He interprets
Elizabeth Willard's statement--"I wanted to run away from
everything, but I wanted to run toward something, too"--as
central to Anderson's main theme: "There is, on the one
hand, the desire to escape from the walls of self; ... on the
other, there is the desire to fly toward some kind of un-
nameable spiritual union with God, man, or nature" (112).

630. Walcutt, Charles Child. "SA: Impressionism and the
Buried Life." American Literary Naturalism: A
Divided Stream. Minneapolis: The University of
Minnesota Press, 1956, pp. 222-39.
Walcutt's thesis that naturalism is the offspring
of transcendentalism forms the context in which he considers
elements of naturalism in Winesburg. He suggests that Anderson explores two major themes: discovery and inhibition.
"The theme of discovery is the recognition of the Spirit, the
unfolding of the world and its perception by the intuition, the
secret insight by which man's life is suddenly revealed to
him." Such a moment of discovery comes for George Willard
in "Sophistication." The second theme, inhibition, appears
in almost all of Anderson's stories. It relates to three broad
areas of cause and experience: 1) the problem of maturing,
2) frustration resulting from the absence of a tradition of
manners, and 3) the problem of socio-educational opportunity.

631. Winther, S. K. "The Aura of Loneliness in SA."
Modern Fiction Studies, 5 (Summer 1959), pp. 145-
52.
Winther argues that the aura of loneliness is the
chief identifying mark of Anderson's characters, not only in
Winesburg, but in the whole of his work. With the identification of loneliness and isolation Anderson touches upon a

fact of nature that is both empirically true and true in terms of his fiction. The theme of isolation recurs throughout Anderson's novels and short stories constituting "a conscious attempt on his part to present an aspect of life that he considered universal" (148). Winther documents his argument with special reference to Winesburg, Windy McPherson's Son, Tar, and other works.

(Further references: 375, 376, 377, 379, 380, 382, 387, 408, 420, 422, 424, 425, 427, 430, 433, 434, 438, 444, 445, 446, 447, 448, 453, 454, 456, 458, 460, 462, 463, 464, 466, 468, 471, 472, 473, 475, 479, 483, 485, 486, 491, 498, 500, 508, 509, 513, 518, 524.)

E. BIBLIOGRAPHIES

632.   Aldridge, John W., ed. Critiques and Essays on Modern Fiction 1920-51. New York: Ronald Press Company, 1952, pp. 572-74.

633.   Gozzi, Raymond D. "A Bibliography of SA's Contributions to Periodicals, 1914-1946." Newberry Library Bulletin, Second Series, No. 2 (December 1948), pp. 71-82.

634.   Jessup, Mary E. "A Checklist of the Writings of SA." American Collector, 5 (January 1928), pp. 157-58.

635.   Johnson, Merle D. American First Editions, 4th ed. by Jacob Blanck. New York: Bowker, 1942, pp. 25-27.

636.   Johnson, Richard C. "Addenda to Sheehy and Lohf's Bibliography of SA." Papers of the Bibliographical Society of America, 66 (January-March 1972), p. 61.

637.   "Library Notes." Newberry Library Bulletin, 6 (November 1962), p. 32.

638.   Sheehy, Eugene P. and Kenneth A. Lohf. SA: A Bibliography. Los Gatos, California: Talisman Press, 1960.

639.   Tanselle, G. Thomas.   "Additional Reviews of SA's
       Work. "   Papers of the Bibliographical Society of
       America, 56 (Third Quarter 1962), pp. 358-65.

640.   _____ .   "The First Notice of SA. "   Notes and
       Queries, 9 (August 1962), pp. 307-09.

641.   _____ .   [Review of SA: A Bibliography.]   Wisconsin
       Studies in Contemporary Literature, 3 (Fall 1962), pp.
       106-12.

642.   White, Ray Lewis.   Checklist of SA.   Columbus,
       Ohio: Charles E. Merrill, 1969.

643.   _____ .   "A Checklist of SA Studies, 1959-1969. "
       Newberry Library Bulletin, 6, No. 8 (July 1971), pp.
       288-302.

                F.   Ph. D. DISSERTATIONS (UNPUBLISHED)

644.   Anderson, David D.   "SA and the Meaning of the
       American Experience. "   Michigan State University,
       1960.

645.   Carlson, G. Bert, Jr.   "SA's Political Mind: The
       Activist Years. "   University of Maryland, 1966.

646.   Cole, Janis Ellen.   "Many Marriages: SA's Con-
       troversial Novel. "   University of Chicago, 1965.

647.   Crist, Robert L.   "SA's Dark Laughter: Sources,
       Composition, and Reputation. "   University of Chicago,
       1966.

648.   Curry, Martha M.   "The 'Writer's Book' by SA: A
       Critical Edition. "   Loyola University of Chicago, 1972.

649.   Fanning, Michael W.   "France and SA. "   University
       of Arkansas, 1971.

650.   Ferres, John Howard.   "The Right Place and the Right
       People: SA's Search for Salvation. "   Louisiana State
       University, 1959.

651. Finkel, Jan M. "Techniques in Portraying the Gro-
      tesque in Selected Writings of Nathaniel Hawthorne,
      SA, and Joseph Heller. " Indiana University, 1974.

652. Hart, Robert C. "Writers on Writing: the Opinions
      of Six Modern American Novelists on the Craft of
      Fiction. " Northwestern University, 1954.

653. Hilton, Earl R. "The Purpose and Method of SA. "
      University of Minnesota, 1950.

654. Hipkiss, Robert A. "The Value of Expatriation for
      the Major American Novelists. " University of Cali-
      fornia at Los Angeles, 1966.

655. Klein, Marie A. "The Stalled Traveler: A New Ap-
      proach to the Full-Length Works of SA. " University
      of Illinois, 1973.

656. Kraft, Robert G. "SA, Bisexual Bard: Some Chap-
      ters in a Literary Biography. " University of Wash-
      ington, 1969.

657. Lemmon, Dallas M. "The Rovelle, or the Novel of
      Interrelated Stories: M. Lermontov, G. Keller, SA. "
      Indiana University, 1970.

658. Love, Glen A. "SA's American Pastoral. " Univer-
      sity of Washington, 1964.

659. Menkin, Gabriel A. "Structure in SA's Fiction. "
      University of Pittsburgh, 1968.

660. Miller, William V. "The Technique of SA's Short
      Stories. " University of Illinois, 1968.

661. Nemanic, Gerald C. "Talbot Whittingham: An An-
      notated Edition of the Text with a Descriptive and
      Critical Essay. " University of Arizona, 1969.

662. Phillips, William L. "SA's Winesburg, Ohio: Its
      Origins, Composition, Technique, and Reception. "
      University of Chicago, 1950.

663. Potter, Hugh M. , III. "The 'Romantic Nationalists'
      of the 1920's. " University of Minnesota, 1964.

664.   Rothweiler, Robert L.   "Ideology and Four Radical
        Novelists: The Response to Communism of Dreiser,
        Anderson, Dos Passos, and Farrell. " Washington
        University, 1960.

665.   Sebastion, Dillard F. , Jr.   "SA's Theory of Art. "
        Louisiana State University, 1972.

666.   Silverman, Raymond J.   "The Short Story Composite:
        Forms, Functions, and Applications. " University of
        Michigan, 1970.

667.   Somers, Paul P. , Jr.   "SA and Ernest Hemingway:
        Influences and Parallels. "   Penn State University,
        1970.

668.   Sullivan, Barbara W. "A Gallery of Grotesques:
        The Alienation Theme in the Works of Hawthorne,
        Twain, Anderson, Faulkner, and Wolfe. " University
        of Georgia, 1969.

669.   Sutton, William A.   "SA's Formative Years: 1876-
        1913. "   Ohio State University, 1943.

670.   Taylor, Welford D.   "SA's 'Buck Fever': A Critical
        Edition. " University of Maryland, 1966.

671.   Thissen, John H.   "SA and Painting. " Northwestern
        University, 1974.

672.   Thurston, Jarvis A.   "SA: A Critical Study. "   State
        University of Iowa, 1946.

673.   White, Ray Lewis.   "SA's Marching Men: The Genetic
        Manuscript Text. " University of Arkansas, 1971.

674.   Yancy, Anita V. R.   'Winesburg, Ohio and The
        Pastures of Heaven: A Comparative Analysis of Two
        Studies of Isolation. " University of Southern Missis-
        sippi, 1971.

G. BOOK REVIEWS

Beyond Desire (1932)

675.   Chamberlain, John. New York Times Book Review
        (25 September 1932), p. 6.

676.   Dawson, Margaret C. New York Herald Tribune
        Books (25 September 1932), p. 7.

677.   Fadiman, Clifton. Nation, 135 (2 November 1932),
        pp. 432-33.

678.   Herring, Marriet L. Journal of Social Forces, 11
        (December 1932), pp. 295-98.

679.   Hicks, Granville. New Republic, 73 (21 December
        1932), pp. 168-69.

680.   Whipple, T. K. Saturday Review of Literature, 9
        (10 December 1932), p. 305.

Dark Laughter (1925)

681.   Boyd, Ernest. Independent, 115 (12 September 1925),
        p. 302.

682.   Brickell, Herschel. Bookman, 62 (November 1925),
        pp. 338-39.

683.   Butcher, Fanny. Chicago Tribune (10 October 1925),
        p. 14.

684.   Canby, Henry S. Saturday Review of Literature, 2
        (10 October 1925), p. 191.

685.   Kennedy, P. C. New Statesman, 27 (5 June 1926),
        p. 199.

686.   Krutch, Joseph Wood. Nation, 121 (2 December
        1925), pp. 626-27.

687.   Lanfeld, William R. Literary Digest International

Book Review, 3 (November 1925), pp. 805, 808.

688. Lovett, Robert Morss. New Republic, 44 (21 October 1925), pp. 233-34.

689. MacLeish, Archibald. Atlantic Monthly, 137 (December 1925), p. 14.

690. Mencken, H. L. American Mercury, 6 (November 1925), pp. 379-80.

691. Sherman, Stuart P. New York Herald Tribune Books (4 October 1925), p. 1.

692. Yust, Walter. New York Evening Post Literary Review (26 September 1925), p. 2.

Death in the Woods and Other Stories (1933)

693. Chamberlain, John. Saturday Review of Literature, 9 (29 April 1933), p. 561.

694. Hansen, Harry. New York World-Telegram (15 April 1933), p. 13.

695. Kronenberger, Louis. New York Times Book Review (23 April 1933), p. 6.

696. Marsh, F. T. New York Herald Tribune Books (16 April 1933), p. 4.

697. Mathews, T. S. New Republic, 75 (7 June 1933), pp. 105-06.

698. Mellquist, Jerome. Commonweal, 18 (7 July 1933), p. 273.

699. Troy, William. Nation, 136 (3 May 1933), p. 508.

Hello Towns! (1929)

700. Brooks, Walter R. Outlook, 152 (8 May 1929), p. 78.

701.   Edgett, E. F.   Boston Transcript (27 April 1929), p. 3.

702.   Gannett, Lewis.   New York Herald Tribune Books (5 May 1929), p. 3.

703.   Haardt, Sara.   Saturday Review of Literature, 5 (4 May 1929), p. 974.

704.   Hellman, Geoffrey.   New Republic, 58 (15 May 1929), p. 365.

705.   Hutchison, Percy.   New York Times Book Review (28 April 1929), p. 1.

706.   Mencken, H. L.   American Mercury, 17 (June 1929), pp. 254-54.

707.   White, William A.   Nation, 128 (12 June 1929), p. 714.

Home Town (1940)

708.   Canby, Henry S.   Saturday Review of Literature, 23 (11 January 1941), p. 21.

709.   Cort, John C.   Commonweal, 33 (20 December 1940), p. 233.

710.   Crandell, R. F.   New York Herald Tribune Books (27 October 1940), p. 5.

711.   Duffus, R. L.   New York Times Book Review (27 October 1940), p. 1.

712.   Gannett, Lewis.   Boston Transcript (23 October 1940), p. 11.

713.   Kellogg, Florence L.   Survey Graphic, 29 (December (1940), pp. 635, 637.

714.   New Yorker, 16 (2 November 1940), p. 87.

715.   Thompson, Ralph.   New York Times (22 October 1940), p. 21.

716.   Time, 36 (28 October 1940), pp. 60-61.

Horses and Men (1923)

717.   Arvin, Newton. Freeman, 8 (5 December 1923), pp. 307-08.

718.   Collins, Joseph. Literary Digest International Book Review, 2 (December 1923), p. 42.

719.   Gregory, Alyse. New York Evening Post Literary Review (8 December 1923), p. 333.

720.   Lewisohn, Ludwig. Nation, 118 (30 April 1924), pp. 510-11.

721.   Littell, Robert. New Republic, 37 (19 December 1923), pp. 99-100.

722.   Lovett, Robert Morss. Dial, 76 (March 1924), pp. 274-76.

723.   Mencken, H. L. American Mercury, 1 (February 1924), p. 252.

724.   New York Times Book Review (25 November 1923), pp. 7, 25.

725.   Rascoe, Burton. New York Tribune Book News and Reviews (25 November 1923), p. 20.

Kit Brandon (1936)

726.   Basso, Hamilton. New Republic, 88 (21 October 1936), p. 318.

727.   Book Buyer, 2, No. 8 (Christmas 1936), p. 9.

728.   Jones, Howard Mumford. Saturday Review of Literature. 14 (10 October 1936), p. 13.

729.   Kazin, Alfred. New York Herald Tribune Books (11 October 1936), p. 1.

730. Stone, Geoffrey. Commonweal, 25 (20 November 1936), p. 109.

731. Time, 28 (12 October 1936), p. 87.

732. Van Doren, Mark. Nation, 143 (17 October 1936), pp. 452-53.

733. Young, Stanley. New York Times Book Review (11 October 1936), p. 3.

Letters of SA (1953)

734. Flanagan, John T. Southwest Review, 38 (Autumn 1953), pp. xiv-xv, 350.

735. Hardwick, Elizabeth. Partisan Review, 20 (November 1953), pp. 690-92.

736. Miller, Perry. New Republic, 128 (22 June 1953), pp. 19-20.

737. Paulding, Gouverneur. Reporter, 8 (23 June 1953), pp. 38-39.

738. Raymund, Bernard. Arizona Quarterly, 9 (Winter 1953), pp. 357-59.

739. Thorp, Willard. Nation, 176 (20 June 1953), pp. 526-28.

740. Weber, Brom. Saturday Review, 36 (20 June 1953), p. 20.

Many Marriages (1923)

741. Boynton, H. W. Independent, 110 (31 March 1923), p. 232.

742. Broun, Heywood. New York World (25 February 1923), Section E., p. 6.

743. Canby, Henry S. New York Evening Post Literary

Review (24 Feburary 1923), p. 483.

744. Gould, Gerald. Saturday Review, 136 (8 September 1923), p. 281.

745. Jones, Llewellyn. Chicago Evening Post Literary Review (2 March 1923).

746. Lewisohn, Ludwig. Nation, 116 (28 March 1923), p. 368.

747. Littell, Robert. New Republic, 37 (11 April 1923), pp. 6-8.

748. Mencken, H. L. Smart Set, 71 (July 1923), pp. 138-39.

749. New York Times Book Review (25 February 1923), p. 10.

750. Rascoe, Burton. New York Tribune Book News and Reviews (25 February 1923), p. 17.

751. Stone, Percy N. Bookman, 57 (April 1923), pp. 210-11.

752. Wilson, Edmund. Dial, 74 (April 1923), pp. 399-400.

Marching Men (1917)

753. Boynton, H. W. Bookman, 46 (November 1917), p. 338.

754. Donlin, George B. Dial, 63 (27 September 1917), pp. 274-75.

755. Hackett, Francis. New Republic, 12 (29 September 1917), pp. 249-50.

756. Mencken, H. L. Smart Set, 53 (December 1917), p. 143.

757. New York Times Book Review (28 October 1917), p. 442.

758.   Webb, Doris. Publishers' Weekly, 92 (20 October
        1917), p. 1372.

                        Mid-American Chants (1918)

759.   Conkling, Grace H.   Yale Review, 8 (January 1919),
        pp. 437-38.

760.   Henderson, A. C.   Poetry, 12 (June 1918), pp. 155-
        58.

761.   Jones, Llewellyn.   Chicago Evening Post (26 April
        1918), p. 10.

762.   New Republic, 17 (4 January 1919), pp. 288-89.

763.   Untermeyer, Louis.   Dial, 64 (23 May 1918), pp.
        483-85.

764.   Walsh, Thomas.   Bookman, 47 (August 1918), pp.
        641-42.

                        The Modern Writer (1925)

765.   Bookman, 63 (May 1926), p. 361.

766.   Fagin, N. Bryllion.   Literary Digest International
        Book Review, 4 (August 1926), p. 593.

767.   New York Times Book Review (10 January 1926), p.
        14.

                        A New Testament (1927)

768.   Aiken, Conrad.   New York Evening Post Literary
        Review (9 July 1927), p. 8.

769.   Deutsch, Babette.   New York Herald Tribune Books
        (24 July 1927), p. 2.

770.   Farrar, John.   Bookman, 65 (August 1927), p. 710.

771. Hansen, Harry. New York World (19 June 1927),
      Section M, p. 8.

772. Miles, Hamish. Saturday Review of Literature, 4
      (3 September 1927), p. 85.

773. New York Times Book Review (12 June 1927), p. 9.

Perhaps Women (1931)

774. Canby, Henry S. Saturday Review of Literature, 8
      (10 October 1931), p. 183.

775. Feld, R. C. New York Times Book Review (27
      September 1931), p. 2.

776. Forum, 86 (November 1931), pp. vi, viii.

777. Godwin, Murray. New Republic, 69 (18 November
      1931), pp. 24-25.

778. Gregory, Horace. Nation, 133 (14 October 1931),
      pp. 401-02.

779. Hansen, Harry. New York World-Telegram (15 Sep-
      tember 1931), p. 25.

780. Nelson, John C. Survey, 67 (1 February 1932), pp.
      498-99.

781. Ross, Mary. New York Herald Tribune Books (20
      September 1931), p. 5.

782. Salpeter, Harry. Outlook, 159 (7 October 1931), p.
      184.

Plays: Winesburg and Others (1937)

783. Eaton, W. P. New York Herald Tribune Books (31
      October 1937), p. 22.

784. Jack, P. M. New York Times Book Review (14
      November 1937), p. 9.

785.   Theatre Arts Monthly, 21 (October 1937), pp. 824-
       25.

                         Poor White (1920)

786.   Benchley, Robert C.   Bookman, 52 (February 1921),
       pp. 559-60.

787.   Gershom, Eric.   Publishers' Weekly, 98 (18 Decem-
       ber 1920), p. 1888.

788.   Hackett, Francis.   New Republic, 24 (24 November
       1920), p. 330.

789.   Lovett, Robert Morss.   Dial, 70 (January 1921), pp.
       77-79.

790.   Mencken, H. L.   Smart Set, 63 (December 1920), pp.
       138-39.

791.   Nation, 111 (10 November 1920), pp. 536-37.

792.   New York Times Book Review (12 December 1920),
       p. 20.

793.   Peattie, Elia W.   Chicago Tribune (18 December
       1920), p. 8.

794.   Rourke, Constance.   New York Evening Post Literary
       Review (4 December 1920), p. 4.

795.   Scott, C. Kay.   Freeman, 2 (5 January 1921), p. 403.

796.   Untermeyer, Louis.   Liberator, 4 (February 1921), pp.
       32-34.

                       The Portable SA (1949)

797.   Klein, Alexander.   New Republic, 121 (15 August
       1949), pp. 18-19.

798.   Redman, Ben Ray.   Saturday Review of Literature, 32
       (23 April 1949), p. 40.

799. Time, 53 (28 February 1949), pp. 96, 98, 100.

Puzzled America (1935)

800. Adamic, Louis. Saturday Review of Literature, 11 (13 April 1935), p. 621.

801. Basso, Hamilton. New Republic, 82 (1 May 1935), p. 348.

802. Bates, Ernest S. New York Herald Tribune Books (7 April 1935), p. 5.

803. Davidson, Donald. American Review, 5 (May 1935), pp. 234-38.

804. Duffus, R. L. New York Times Book Review (7 April 1935), p. 1.

805. Gannett, Lewis. New York Herald Tribune Books (30 March 1935), p. 9.

806. Literary Digest, 119 (6 April 1935), p. 26.

807. MacCampbell, Donald. Atlantic Monthly, 156 (August 1935), p. 10.

808. Stein, Gertrude. Chicago Daily Tribune (4 May 1935), p. 14.

The SA Reader (1947)

809. Bailey, Robeson. Saturday Review of Literature, 30 (6 December 1947), p. 52.

810. Cowley, Malcolm. New York Herald Tribune Weekly Book Review (9 November 1947), pp. 1-2.

811. Dupee, F. W. Nation, 166 (3 January 1948), p. 20.

812. Hoffman, Frederick J. American Literature, 20 (March 1948), pp. 73-74.

813.   Howe, Irving. Partisan Review, 15 (April 1948),
        pp. 492-99.

814.   Stevenson, Lionel. Personalist, 29 (October 1948),
        pp. 426-27.

815.   Trilling, Lionel. New York Times Book Review (9
        November 1947), pp. 1, 67-69.

        SA/Gertrude Stein: Correspondence
               and Personal Essays (1972)

816.   Cash, E. A. Best Sellers, 32 (15 March 1973), p.
        564.

817.   Choice, 10 (May 1973), p. 452.

818.   Fraser, R. S. Library Journal, 97 (1 December
        1972), p. 3911.

819.   New York Times Book Review (8 April 1973), p. 30.

820.   Virginia Quarterly Review, 49 (Spring 1973), p. lxxvi.

        SA's Memoirs (1942)

821.   Chamberlain, John. New York Times (9 April 1942),
        p. 17.

822.   Dell, Floyd. New York Herald Tribune Books (12
        April 1942), pp. 1-2.

823.   Duffus, R. L. New York Times Book Review (12
        April 1942), p. 3.

824.   Geismar, Maxwell. Yale Review, N. S. 32 (Autumn
        1942), pp. 183-85.

825.   Gissen, Max. New Republic, 106 (20 April 1942),
        pp. 548-49.

826.   Hansen, Harry. Saturday Review of Literature, 25
        (11 April 1942), pp. 5-6.

827. Isherwood, Christopher. Partisan Review, 9 (July-August 1942), pp. 341-42.

828. Marshall, Margaret. Nation, 154 (16 May 1942), p. 574.

829. New Yorker, 18 (11 April 1942), p. 87.

830. Paulding, J. K. Commonweal, 36 (24 April 1942), pp. 19-20.

831. Sutton, William A. Historical Society of Northwestern Ohio Quarterly Bulletin, 14 (July 1942), pp. 109-11.

SA's Memoirs: A Critical Edition (1969)

832. Connell, E. S. New York Times Book Review (10 August 1969).

833. Junker, Howard. New Yorker, 45 (18 October 1969), p. 215.

834. Newsweek, 74 (25 August 1969), p. 82.

835. Rideout, Walter B. Virginia Quarterly Review, 45 (Summer 1969), p. 537.

836. Thompson, R. J. Library Journal, 94 (15 May 1969), p. 1890.

837. Turner, S. J. American Scholar, 39 (Winter 1969),

838. Weber, Brom. Saturday Review, 52 (23 August 1969), p. 38.

SA's Notebook (1926)

839. Brock, H. I. New York Times Book Review (9 May 1926), p. 2.

840. Brooks, Van Wyck. Forum, 76 (October 1926), p. 637.

841.   Colton, Arthur. Saturday Review of Literature, 2
        (17 July 1926), p. 933.

842.   Cuppy, Will. Bookman, 63 (July 1926), pp. 599-600.

843.   Deutsch, Babette. New York Herald Tribune Books
        (20 June 1926), p. 7.

844.   Dial, 82 (January 1927), p. 751.

845.   Ford, James L. Literary Digest International Book
        Review, 4 (September 1926), pp. 654-55.

846.   Hansen, Harry. New York World (9 May 1926), Sec-
        tion M, p. 6.

847.   Independent, 116 (26 June 1926), p. 751.

848.   Nation, 123 (18 August 1926), p. 155.

849.   Outlook, 143 (21 July 1926), p. 420.

850.   Yust, Walter. New York Evening Post Literary Re-
        view (22 May 1926), p. 3.

A Story Teller's Story (1924)

851.   Benet, William R. Saturday Review of Literature,
        1 (18 October 1924), p. 200.

852.   Bromfield, Louis. Bookman, 60 (December 1924),
        pp. 492-93.

853.   Gorman, Herbert S. Literary Digest International
        Book Review, 2 (December 1924), pp. 15-16.

854.   Hansen, Harry. Nation, 119 (10 December 1924),
        pp. 640-41.

855.   Hemingway, Ernest. Ex Libris, 2 (March 1925),
        pp. 176-77.

856.   Kellogg, Arthur. Survey, 53 (1 December 1924),
        pp. 288-89.

857. Lewis, Sinclair. New York Herald Tribune Books (9 November 1924), pp. 1-2.

858. Lovett, Robert Morss. New Republic, 40 (5 November 1924), pp. 255-56.

859. Morris, Lloyd. New York Times Book Review (12 October 1924), p. 6.

860. Powys, Llewellyn. Dial, 78 (April 1925), pp. 330-32.

861. Stein, Gertrude. Ex Libris, 2 (March 1925), p. 177.

862. Van Doren, Carl. Century, 109 (March 1925), pp. 176-77.

863. Yust, Walter. New York Evening Post Literary Review (1 November 1924), p. 4.

Tar: A Midwest Childhood (1926)

864. Colton, Arthur. Saturday Review of Literature, 3 (19 February 1927), p. 593.

865. Dial, 82 (March 1927), p. 256.

866. Fadiman, Clifton. Nation, 124 (2 February 1927), pp. 121-22.

867. Gorman, H. S. New York World (5 December 1926), Section M, p. 2.

868. Hartley, L. P. Saturday Review, 144 (19 November 1927), p. 709.

869. Mencken, H. L. American Mercury, 10 (March 1927), pp. 382-83.

870. New Statesman, 30 (17 December 1927), pp. 330, 332.

871. New York Evening Post Literary Review (22 January 1927), p. 2.

872. New York World (5 December 1926), Section M, p. 11.

873. Outlook, 154 (12 January 1927), p. 60.

874. West, Rebecca. New York Herald Tribune Books
      (21 November 1926), p. 1.

The Triumph of the Egg (1921)

875. Benet, William R. New York Evening Post Literary
      Review (26 November 1921), p. 200.

876. Broun, Heywood. New York World (6 December 1921),
      p. 11.

877. Colum, Mary M. Freeman, 4 (30 November 1921),
      pp. 281-82.

878. Farrar, John. Bookman, 54 (December 1921), p.
      378.

879. Gilman, Lawrence. North American Review, 216
      (March 1922), pp. 412-16.

880. Hawthorne, Hildegarde. New York Times Book Re-
      view (4 December 1921), p. 10.

881. Lovett, Robert Morss. Dial, 72 (January 1922),
      pp. 79-83.

882. _____. New Republic, 28 (23 November 1921), pp.
      383-84.

883. Mencken, H. L. Smart Set, 67 (February 1922),
      p. 143.

884. Nation, 113 (23 November 1921), p. 602.

Windy McPherson's Son (1916)

885. Boynton, H. W. Bookman, 44 (December 1916),
      pp. 393-94; 45 (May 1917), p. 307.

886. _____. Nation, 103 (30 November 1916), p. 508;
      104 (11 January 1917), pp. 49-50.

887. Dell, Floyd. Masses, 9 (November 1916), p. 17.

888. Frank, Waldo. Seven Arts, 1 (November 1916), pp. 73-78.

889. Hackett, Francis. New Republic, 9 (20 January 1917), pp. 333-36.

890. Heap, Jane. Little Review, 3 (November 1916), pp. 6-7.

891. Hecht, Ben. Chicago Evening Post (8 September 1916), p. 11.

892. Mencken, H. L. Smart Set, 50 (October 1916), p. 144.

893. New York Times Book Review (8 October 1916), p. 423.

894. North American Review, 204 (December 1916), pp. 942-43.

895. Phelps, William Lyon. Dial, 61 (21 September 1916), pp. 196-97.

896. Times Literary Supplement (9 November 1916), p. 536.

Winesburg, Ohio (1919)

897. Boynton, H. W. Bookman, 49 (August 1919), pp. 729-30.

898. Broun, Heywood. New York Tribune (31 May 1919), p. 10.

899. Dell, Floyd. Liberator, 2 (September 1919), pp. 46-47.

900. Dial, 66 (28 June 1919), p. 666.

901. Harris, Frank. Pearson's, 47 (August 1921), pp. 87-88.

902.   Jones, Llewellyn.   Chicago Evening Post (20 June 1919), p. 9.

903.   Mencken, H. L.   Smart Set, 59 (August 1919), pp. 140, 142.

904.   Nation, 108 (28 June 1919), p. 1017.

905.   New Republic, 19 (25 June 1919), pp. 257-60.

906.   New York Sun (1 June 1919), p. 3.

907.   Rascoe, Burton.   Chicago Tribune (7 June 1919), p. 13.

908.   West, Rebecca.   New Statesman, 19 (22 July 1922), pp. 443-44.

APPENDIX

BIBLIOGRAPHY
(A List of References Consulted)

Abstracts of English Studies.

Aldridge, John W. , ed. Critiques and Essays on Modern
Fiction 1920-51. New York: Ronald Press Company,
1952, pp. 572-74.

American Literary Scholarship. An Annual.

American Literature (Bibliography).

Annual Bibliography of English Language and Literature.
Marjory Rigby, et al. , eds. Cambridge, England:
Modern Humanities Research Association.

Bibliographic Index.

Biography Index.

Book Review Digest.

Book Review Index.

Books in Print.

Cumulative Book Index.

Current Biography.

Dissertation Abstracts.

Dissertation Abstracts International.

Dissertations in American Literature, 1891-1955; Supplement, 1956-61, by James Woodress. Durham, North

Carolina: Duke University Press, 1962.

Essay and General Literature Index.

Gozzi, Raymond D.   "A Bibliography of SA's Contributions
   to Periodicals, 1914-1946. " Newberry Library Bulletin,
   Second Series, No. 2 (December 1948), pp. 71-82.

Jessup, Mary E.   "A Checklist of the Writings of SA. "
   American Collector, 5 (January 1928), pp. 157-58.

Johnson, Merle D.   American First Editions, 4th ed. by
   Jacob Blanck.   New York: Bowker, 1942, pp. 25-27.

Johnson, Richard C.   "Addenda to Sheehy and Lohf's Bibliography of SA. " Papers of the Bibliographical Society
   of America, 66 (January-March 1972), p. 61.

"Library Notes. " Newberry Library Bulletin, 6 (November
   1962), p. 32.

The Library of Congress Catalog of Printed Cards.

A Library of Literary Criticism: Modern American Literature.

Modern Language Association Bibliography.

The National Union Catalog.

Readers' Guide to Periodical Literature.

Sheehy, Eugene P. and Kenneth A. Lohf.   SA: A Bibliography.   Los Gatos, California: Talisman Press, 1960.

Short Story Index.

Tanselle, G. Thomas.   "Additional Reviews of SA's Work. "
   Papers of the Bibliographical Society of America, 56
   (Third Quarter 1962), pp. 358-65.

_____.   "The First Notice of SA. " Notes and Queries,
   9 (August 1962), pp. 307-09.

Twentieth Century Authors, With Supplements.

White, Ray Lewis. <u>Checklist of SA.</u> Columbus, Ohio: Charles E. Merrill, 1969.

_____. "A Checklist of SA Studies, 1959-1969." <u>Newberry Library Bulletin</u>, 6, No. 8 (July 1971), pp. 288-302.

AUTHOR INDEX